Editor
Jennifer Prior, Ed. D.

Managing Editor
Ina Massler Levin, M.A.

Editor-in-Chief
Sharon Coan, M.S. Ed.

Illustrators
Kevin Barnes
Brenda DiAntonis
Howard Chaney

Cover Artist
Brenda DiAntonis

Art Manager
Kevin Barnes

Imaging
Ralph Olmedo, Jr.
Rosa C. See

Product Manager
Phil Garcia

Publishers
Rachelle Cracchiolo, M.S. Ed.
Mary Dupuy Smith, M.S. Ed.

LITERACY
THROUGH
Dramatic Play Centers

Author

Mara Ellen Guckian

Teacher Created Materials, Inc.
6421 Industry Way
Westminster, CA 92683
www.teachercreated.com
ISBN-0-7439-3378-8
©*2004 Teacher Created Materials, Inc.*
Made in U.S.A.

Table of Contents

Introduction

The educational requirements placed on educators of young children have increased dramatically as a result of state and national standards and testing programs. Literacy and numeracy skills are now required at a much earlier age, causing many preschool and early primary programs to reexamine their curriculum. No one wants to give up hands-on experiences in music, science, art, drama, or free play, but fitting everything into a day, a week, or even a year can be difficult. Educators need to create positive, well-rounded learning experiences filled with numeracy and literacy activities. They must also create situations in which children can practice a variety of social skills and communication skills, such as sharing, being flexible, negotiating, and taking turns. Most importantly, educators need to maintain a stimulating, challenging environment in which children can practice these many skills.

The pressure to push children to meet arbitrary performance standards is great. The guidelines have become rigid timetables instead of goals to be mastered as a child matures. How can we help young children learn skills in a developmentally appropriate manner? Simple, young children learn by doing. They learn through play, through experimentation, and by exercising their imaginations. Each day, children build on the experiences of the day before. Sometimes they are ready to move on to the next level quickly, and sometimes they need more practice with the same activity. For each child the timetable is different, but for all, it takes practice to master a skill or a concept, and practice to make it real. Once a skill is real to a child and integrated into his/her knowledge base, performance can be measured.

For young children, mimicking the world around them is one way in which they absorb information. Dramatic play is a lot more than a box of dress-up clothes in a corner. Through the dramas children initiate, they learn to make sense of their world. They learn to interact with their peers. They develop language and social skills. They become aware of numbers and words, reading and writing, and other forms of communication. By creating and manipulating their props, they develop fine and gross motor skills. They learn to share and to negotiate. Dramatic play offers children a safe way to explore their world and to try out new ideas.

The dramatic play themes suggested in this book are divided into indoor and outdoor centers, but all can be done indoors. When an outdoor center is underway, more emphasis will be placed on verbal and listening skills. However, suggestions are given for related activities that can be done in the classroom to reinforce the concepts. For the most part, the centers are recreations of places children frequent with their families. A few centers offer views into worlds not a part of most of our everyday lives, but they are very exciting nonetheless. By creating different, real-life scenarios, the larger world comes to children a little bit at a time. In turn, they use their imaginations and creativity to expand the concepts being presented to them. Literacy and numeracy skills, practiced as a part of "real-life" situations, become real to children.

Literacy Through Dramatic Play Centers offers educators and their students many exciting opportunities to explore the world from their very own rooms. Children can take on new roles and interact as different characters through the props, writing materials, and manipulatives provided. Dramatic play offers educators a method of challenging children to learn through practical experience. Dramatic play is esteem-building, educational, and fun!

How to Use This Book

Involve Children in the Process

Plan to change the dramatic play center every few weeks. Encourage children to help with each center's preparation. Children can help gather and put away old materials in anticipation of each new center. Cleaning up and caring for the environment are important skills to incorporate into every activity. Children can also help create signs and post labels for the next area scheduled.

Encourage their participation during a "planning" time. Refer to it as a "business meeting" and you will be surprised at how important children feel and how willing they are to participate. Explain that you want their help to design a new area in the classroom. For instance, suppose you are dismantling the existing Housekeeping Area. You might ask that each child bring down two food items, or three dishes, or a dress-up item that he or she can carefully fold and place in the storage bin. Someone else might be in charge of collecting the labels in the area. Review the labels as a group. Count the labels before putting them in the storage container. Then, tell them the title of the new area and ask for ideas. As the ideas build, create a list of new labels that will be needed.

Pique the Children's Interest

Each dramatic play center is presented in a similar manner. The first section is entitled *Lead Ins*. Here, suggestions for introducing each new topic are offered. These may include questions to broach, props to share, or a new series of word or picture cards. It might even be a guessing game. The key is to stimulate the children's interests and then make the concept real for them by involving them in the planning. Circle or a whole-group time is best for sharing this information and for getting feedback. Keep in mind, some of the most imaginative ideas for individual centers may come from the creative minds of your young children. Listen to their experiences and incorporate them in the scenarios.

Whenever possible, share authentic items that will be used in the new center. Safety goggles for the Repair Shop or a scuba tank for the Ocean Adventure will certainly spark some lively conversations. Gathering authentic items is an ongoing process and well worth the time and effort.

Supplement the *Lead Ins* with a related story or informational book. Plan on one or two days of lead-in activities before construction of the center begins.

How to Use This Book (cont.)

Make the Creation of Each Dramatic Play Center a Team Effort

The section entitled "Student Preparation" will offer suggestions for activities children can do in advance. Generally, this will include creating a new sign for the area, making props, and gathering materials. Once the center is underway, more center-specific items will be made. Children might determine that they need to have make-believe money, For Sale signs, or price tags. Be sure to keep the writing/craft area well stocked with markers, pens, glue, scissors, yarn scraps, cardboard, and construction paper as children work on creating these props.

The bulk of the preparation will be detailed in the "Teacher Preparation" section. Labels will need to be made, furniture rearranged or remodeled, and props introduced. Where applicable, worksheets may serve to reinforce skills practiced at certain centers. Make extra copies of these to put out as needed.

You will need to create specific labels for each center. Some generic labels are offered in the Appendix. The labels will be determined by the materials and furnishings accumulated for each dramatic play center. Character nametags are offered for each theme. You will also need to determine the number of copies to make and if additional nametags are required. Lamination is suggested for the labels, character nametags, and many of the props to increase durability. If a laminator is not available, clear, adhesive shelf paper can be used. Be sure to laminate or cover both sides of the item.

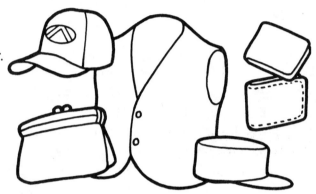

Simple costumes will enhance dramatic play in the centers. Employees in shops can wear hats, caps, vests, and aprons. Patterns for vests and aprons are available in the Appendix on pages 251 and 252. Begin collecting hats, baseball caps, painters' caps, and men's and women's vests. These can all be embellished easily with tape labels, nametags, or other decorative items. Ask local storeowners to donate extra nametags or hats. Additional items for specific dramatic play centers may be listed but the generic items above can be used in many of the centers. Many of the centers involve sales. Encourage "shoppers" and "customers" to wear their own clothes or make use of the regular dress-up attire in the classroom.

Parents can be enlisted to help, too, especially if they work in fields related to a particular center. The more authentic the materials, the more inspired the children will be to use the dramatic play center. The list of materials provides suggestions for items to include in a center. It is not necessary for all items to be included.

Send letters home a week or two before the opening of each play center. Review the suggested materials for each center and request the materials you think you can use. You may be surprised at the support you receive once parents understand the value of your centers. Involve neighborhood stores and civic organizations in the process as well. Often they have materials set aside for school groups or materials they can no longer use. Local copy stores are great sources for paper, envelopes, and boxes. (Be sure to ask for printing mistakes, too.)

How to Use This Book (cont.)

Capitalize on the Literacy and Numeracy Development

The numeracy and literacy development sections offer ideas for incorporating practice in basic skills. Whenever possible, offer opportunities to read and write, and to count, even if children are at the pre-literacy phase. The suggested list of vocabulary words for each dramatic play station includes some of the roles that can be dramatized as well as some of the materials that can be used to make the theme come to life. When introducing these terms, spend time sounding out the words, clapping and counting the syllables, rhyming, etc. Many of the words will be used in spoken vocabulary in the centers. Incorporate these as often as possible in conversations, songs, and stories.

Encourage the children to make a sign to indicate the name of each dramatic play literacy center. There are a number of ways to make these signs once a name has determined. Try these to get started.

> —Write the center name on a large sheet of bulletin-board (butcher) paper using large outlines of letters. Invite children to color in the letters and decorate the background. The letters can also be cut out and glued onto a brightly colored sheet of bulletin-board paper.

> —Have children cut out different pictures of items common to the new center and glue them on a collage. Coupons can be used as a background for the grocery story, travel brochures for air travel, or empty seed packets for the flower and garden shops. Large black letters can be cut out and used to spell the name of the center and children can glue them atop the collage.

> —Spell out the letters in the name of the center by using objects from the center theme. Tongue depressors and cotton swabs could be used for the letters of a Doctor's Office center. Gauze could be used for the Hospital center. Nuts and bolts could be used for the title of the Fix-it Shop.

Environmental print such as signs, labels, and character nametags are important to literacy development. The more children are involved in the creation and review of these items, the better. Each center will have different props, but all will have labels of some kind and all will have different roles to play. In an effort to make role-playing a little easier, character nametags should be provided for each center to identify specific roles. Nametags can be copied on colored paper, cut out, and used as is, or they can be enlarged before laminating. A third option is to place the nametags on larger pieces of construction paper before laminating. Additional nametags and labels can be found in the Appendix on pages 253–256. All nametags should be laminated for durability. Punch holes in the corners and string a length of yarn through the holes in order to create nametags that can be worn around the neck.

Children will soon be "reading" the cards to determine their chosen roles. Inevitably, some roles will be more popular than others. Determine ahead of time how long a child can participate in a specific role before trading with another person. Establish a system to keep track. Use a timer or other method to determine the length of time.

Numbers can be posted at the entrance to the center to indicate how many participants can be in the center at a given time. Use the numeral and a pictogram of some kind to symbolize the number of participants. Creating menus, price sheets, and bills improves literacy and numeracy skills. Introduce the signs for dollar ($) and cents (¢). Begin with pictures and simple number prices and expand to words and numbers with decimal points when appropriate. Practice counting real and play money.

How to Use This Book (cont.)

Capitalize on the Literacy and Numeracy Development (cont.)

Many centers will offer opportunities to weigh and measure using standard or nonstandard measurement tools. Gather an array of scales and measuring cups. Introduce rulers and nonstandard units of measure like a footprint shape.

Involve the children in related cooking activities. Make baked goods for the bakery or restaurant. Scoop and bag snacks for the airplane ride.

Help children prepare make-believe money (pages 246–247), checks (page 249), and credit cards (page 248) for appropriate centers.

Focus on the Drama

Discussing important facts about the theme of a center in your lead-in will help the children in their play. Then it is a good idea for you or another adult to be a part of the drama in the initial days of a new center. Act as a patient in the hospital, a customer in the restaurant, or a pilot on the airplane. Use vocabulary and props as they would be used in a real situation. Be sure not to dominate the play session, however, as this will hinder children's imaginative thinking.

Draw the children's attention to the tasks adults would do in relation to the roles. These can be discussed ahead of time in a group time or after a related book has been read. In a hospital, tasks might include writing prescriptions, measuring medication, and bandaging wounds. If you are playing a customer in the restaurant, you might ask your waiter to tell you what is served. Counting grocery items, adding up bills, and bagging purchases are all activities you and your children can dramatize while in the grocery store center. The possibilities are endless. Draw on your knowledge and your students' experiences to initiate your center and then let their imaginations take over as you distance yourself from active participation.

In some cases, suggested scenarios are included in the Teacher Preparation section or in the Literacy or Numeracy Development sections. These serve as prompts for exploring activities your children might not do on a regular basis with their families. Ideas for traveling on an airplane, scuba diving, or traveling to outer space sometimes need a bit of guidance.

Integrate the Center into other Classroom Activities

Enhance whole-group times with stories, graphing activities, and games related to your theme. Gather related books from the library to share and to place in the centers in waiting rooms, on store shelves, in airplane seats, etc. Plan art, science, movement, and music activities that will complement each center.

If appropriate, have snacks related to the theme. If you are featuring a bakery or restaurant, you might make cupcakes or chips and dip. During the airplane theme, you might have small packets of raisins or pretzels and a variety of beverages.

Periodically, plan field trips related to the featured centers. This opportunity is a wonderful way to expand the experience of each center. Consider scheduling the field trip after the first week the center is available. The children will have had opportunities to use the materials and to familiarize themselves with the new roles and related vocabulary. This will help them to absorb more of the ambiance of the setting. Encourage them to ask questions which can be answered by the "experts."

How to Create a Dramatic Play Area

Your classroom probably has an area set aside for dramatic play. Often, this area is the Housekeeping or Dress-up area but it can be varied to accommodate many other scenarios.

There are a number of ways to create areas within a classroom if a dramatic play area does not exist:

- Create dividers using large pieces of cardboard. Stabilize the cardboard by attaching it to walls or bookshelves with duct tape.

- Use a curtain to create a play area or set up the center inside a tent. A tent can be used for a camping play center, but can also be used to create a play area for an underwater theme.

- Rearrange the furniture to create walls for a center.

- Change wall decorations and posters to reflect the new area. Have children make collages of theme-related magazine pictures. Add appropriate materials. Cut out coupons for the grocery store collage, gauze strips for the hospital collage, or packaging stickers for the post office.

- Reinvent uses for shelves. They can be used as product shelves in a grocery or shoe store, as a cooking or food preparation area in a restaurant, or a supply area in an office center.

- Stack shoeboxes to create miniature shelves, produce racks, hospital chart areas, post office boxes, or office mailboxes.

- Use large appliance boxes (painted by the children) to create ticket booths, fast food counters, post office business windows, rocket ships, or cashier areas.

- Provide library books related to the dramatic play theme. If appropriate, provide brochures, menus, and price sheets from local establishments.

Storing Materials

Gathering props and manipulatives is an important, ongoing process when developing centers. But what do you do with the materials for a center when it is time to move on to the next theme? It is best to determine ahead of time the type of storage that will be necessary. You might want to create a low wall of matching boxes which doubles as a counter or display area or you might make use of classroom shelves.

Use containers that can be stacked on shelves or stored easily in a closet. Ask the manager of a local office supply store or copy center to save the boxes (with lids) used to store reams of paper. These boxes can be labeled and decorated for each center. Their uniform size makes for easy storage of supplies. Another option is to get large plastic containers with flat lids. These too can be labeled and stacked.

It is important to label a box for each center you plan to use. That way, when a new play prop is found, you will know where to store it. You may even find it appropriate to rearrange your center schedule if you find you have received an abundance of items for one center and not enough for another.

Keep a folder in each storage box containing copies of worksheets, small posters, and labels along with lists of consumable materials that will need to be collected next time the center is used. Keep a record of ideas that worked, scenarios that were enacted, and new vocabulary words. Create a list of books that were read (or used as props) and songs or finger plays.

Save your lesson plans and note successful field trips or guest speakers. Tape a list of all the center materials, including items stored elsewhere, to the inside of the box. Add photographs of the center in action.

Note: Actual signs and labels made by the children should not be reused from year to year as the creation of these materials is a part of the literacy component.

Parent Letter

Dear Parents,

Welcome to our class. We are looking forward to a very exciting year and we welcome your participation. We are going to create a dramatic play center in the classroom. Throughout the year, this dramatic play area will be transformed into different themes. It might become a restaurant, a hospital, a space ship, or an underwater paradise! The plan is to change the theme of the area every few weeks to keep the interest level high.

The dramatic play centers will offer children opportunities to work on a variety of important academic and social skills. They will engage in purposeful practice:

- ✔ building vocabulary
- ✔ collaborating
- ✔ counting
- ✔ creating
- ✔ developing phonemic awareness
- ✔ developing print awareness
- ✔ experimenting with materials
- ✔ expressing emotions
- ✔ expressing ideas
- ✔ increasing alphabetic knowledge
- ✔ listening

- ✔ measuring
- ✔ negotiating
- ✔ planning and organizing
- ✔ problem-solving
- ✔ developing reading skills
- ✔ resolving conflicts
- ✔ role-playing
- ✔ sharing
- ✔ taking turns
- ✔ thinking critically
- ✔ writing

Every few weeks a note will be sent home announcing the new theme. We will include a list of suggested items that could be donated. Our goal is to make each center as authentic as possible. Please feel free to suggest something not on the list if you think it will be useful.

We will also be planning field trips and hopefully having a few guests related to our themes. We welcome your suggestions and your help.

Sincerely,

_____

Center Request Letters

Dear Parents,

As you know, we will be rotating dramatic play centers in our classroom this year. There are a number of generic items that will be used in many of the centers. Please keep this list in mind throughout the year. If you have access to any of the items listed below and can donate them it would be greatly appreciated.

- ✔ aprons
- ✔ baseball caps
- ✔ calculators
- ✔ calendar pictures
- ✔ checkbook cases
- ✔ hats of all kinds

- ✔ purses
- ✔ painters' caps
- ✔ scales—all kinds
- ✔ flour sifters
- ✔ colanders
- ✔ shoes—all sizes

- ✔ slippers
- ✔ tote bags
- ✔ twine and rope
- ✔ vests (men's and women's)
- ✔ wallets

Thank you for your help.

Sincerely,

_____

Dear Parents,

It is almost time for a new center in our classroom. The new center will be called_____. The center will open on the following date: _____. If you have any materials you think would be helpful to lend authenticity to our centers, please let us know.

We are particularly looking for the following items:

_____

_____

Thank you again,

Airplane Travel

Lead Ins

- Traveling by airplane may not be a common experience for all children, but it is definitely a center to try. Begin by having the children participate in a simple graphing activity. Draw a graph on the chalkboard or on chart paper. Label one column Yes and the other No. Provide each student with a small airplane cutout. Ask the children if any of them have ever flown in an airplane. Invite each child to attach his or her airplane to the graph under the appropriate heading. Spend time as a group counting and tallying the results of the survey. Write the totals below the graph.

- For another lead in, conduct a discussion about airplanes. How are they different from cars or buses? Compose a Venn diagram to show the differences and similarities between two modes of transportation. Compare ground travel to air travel. Discuss the view from a car as opposed to the view from an airplane. Have the children illustrate what they would view from an airplane.

- Once the subject of airplane travel has been introduced, discuss the process of air travel. Can anyone who can drive a car fly a plane? Who works at an airport and on the plane? Include baggage handlers and checkers, ticket agents, flight crews, security guards, and pilots in the discussion. How does one get a ticket, store luggage, board a plane, etc.? Use your discretion when describing security procedures. Discuss activities for passengers on an airplane, including sleeping, reading, eating, listening to music, and watching movies.

- Introduce books about different types of aircraft. Add stories about traveling in airplanes to the reading area.

- Determine ahead of time if you will be focusing on the whole airport experience or just the plane ride. The information below and on the following pages incorporates the entire air travel experience.

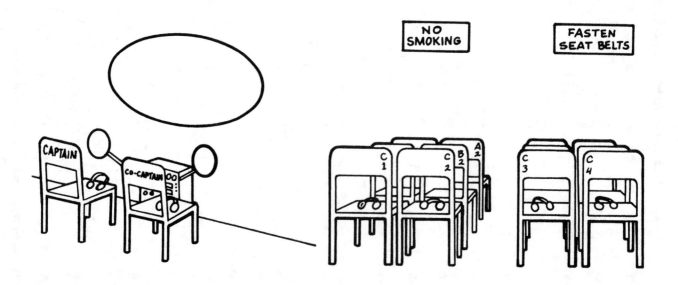

Airplane Travel *(cont.)*

Suggested Materials for Airplane Travel

- airplane pattern
- airplane tickets
- beverage cups
- briefcases
- captain hats
- carry-on luggage that will fit under the classroom chairs
- pipe cleaners or yarn
- chairs
- cloud posters
- discarded computer and keyboards
- empty plastic bottles or cans
- food service items
- head sets
- index cards
- large cardboard box
- maps
- miniature shopping cart
- unused stereo tuners
- oxygen masks
- plastic trays/divided microwave dishes
- purses
- refrigerator box
- roll of pale blue cellophane
- roll of aluminum foil
- scale(s) to weigh suitcases
- suitcases
- travel brochures
- wagon or pull cart for luggage cart
- waxed paper sandwich bags

Airplane Travel (cont.)

Teacher Preparation

Ideally, there will be a ticket purchasing area, a baggage screening area, a boarding area, and a cockpit and seating area on the plane in your dramatic play center.

1. Create a cockpit. Place a large sheet of light blue paper, cut in an oval shape on the wall at eye level to where children will be seated. Beneath it place the student-made control panel. If old stereo equipment with knobs and levers is available, arrange these in front of the control panel on the wall. These will allow children to adjust controls as they fly. A steering wheel would give an added touch of authenticity. If a steering wheel is not available, use a paper plate instead.

2. Arrange two rows of chairs or benches behind the cockpit area. There should be an aisle between the two rows. Place a number on each seat or seat back. Post the NO SMOKING and SEATBELTS ON signs (page 25).

3. Create tickets and boarding passes for each seat on the plane using the templates on pages 22–23. Number each ticket and boarding pass to match a numbered seat on the plane.

4. Create a check-in area. If possible, include a phone, microphone (pattern on page 250), old computer and keyboard, and clipboards. Post a gate number (which can change daily) above the check-in desk. Place stories and books about airplanes in the waiting area.

5. Copy the ticket envelopes onto colored paper matching the colors chosen for the airline. Teach children how to fold on the dashed line to make the ticket envelopes. Place extras in the writing area for children to assemble and decorate.

6. Decorate the classroom with posters of weather conditions, clouds, and different types of aircraft. Display the paper planes created by the children.

7. Consider painting a large picture of a control tower with the children. Display the tower on the wall opposite the airport boarding area. Explain that air traffic controllers work in the tower to guide all the planes in and out safely.

8. Create a security scanner for travelers to walk through using the refrigerator box. See the illustration to the right.

9. Make hats for the captain and co-captain.

10. Make paper vests for the flight attendants. See Appendix, page 251.

11. Label the wagon that will be used to transport luggage.

12. Punch a hole on one side of each of several index cards and loop a pipe cleaner through the hole. These can be used as luggage tags.

13. Convert a child-size stroller or shopping cart into a beverage server for the flight attendants.

14. Use the luggage carrier (wagon) to carry all the lunch boxes for a special luncheon picnic flight.

15. If appropriate, plan a visit to the local airport or invite a person who works in the industry to visit the classroom as a guest speaker.

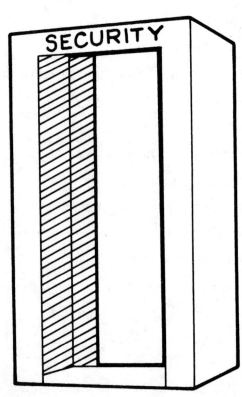

Airplane Travel *(cont.)*

Student Preparation

1. Decide on a name for the airport and create a large sign. Name it after your school, town, city, or state. Write the name of the center in large letter outlines that can be colored in or decorated as desired.

2. Vote on the colors and symbols of the airline. Discuss why each airline has a different look.

3. Create airplanes to match the color scheme chosen. (Enlarge the patterns below.)

4. Review the labels and character nametags. Discuss costume options, such as hats, bandanas, airline pins, etc.

5. Create a control panel for the cockpit, using black or silver tagboard or painted cardboard. Incorporate the gauges on pages 20–21.

6. Decorate the ticket folders (page 22). Simple dot stickers in the appropriate colors will work.

7. Add stickers to the waxed-paper food service bags for decoration. These will be used for "in-flight" snacks.

Airplane Cutouts

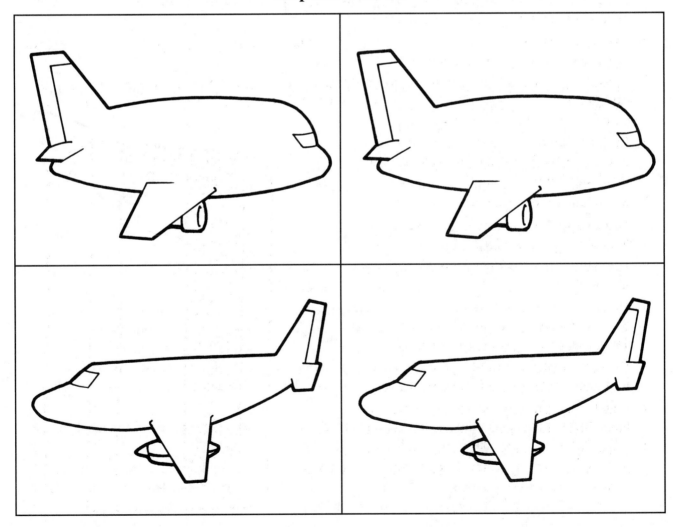

Airplane Travel *(cont)*

Vocabulary Building

air traffic controller	boarding pass	fuel	luggage
airplane	captain	flight attendant	passenger
airport	carry-on	frequent flyer	security
backpacks	cockpit	gate	standby
baggage	duffel bags	gauges	ticket
beverage	first class	guard	

Literacy Development

- Introduce books about air travel and airplanes. Share stories and travel brochures from the reading area. Encourage children to reread the stories to each other during the day.

- Make signs for the airport, the airline, the gate, the ticket booth, the security area, and the baggage claim area.

- Make posters for places the class would like to visit. Add descriptions of the different locations and why they are of interest.

- Create a class book. Have each child write or dictate a story about a plane trip he or she has taken or would like to take in the future. Allow children time to illustrate or add pictures to their pages. Share the book at a discussion time and then make it available in the reading area.

- Discuss all the different words for baggage—luggage, suitcases, carry-ons, backpacks, and duffel bags. What other words can the children think of?

- Discuss all the different jobs at an airport. Add information about each job as books are read and materials are explored. Create new character labels as needed.

- Create a Standby List for children who wish to use the literacy center. Explain that sometimes, they will not make the flight they wish and that they will have to wait until another time or another day for a different flight. Ask if this has ever happened to them or to someone they know. Have them sign in, or, if appropriate, write their names for them. Explain that they will take turns in the order in which their names appear on the list. This is also a good opportunity to work on ordinal numbers.

- Place blank nametags in the writing center. Have children write their names on the labels to use as luggage tags on suitcases.

- Arrange all the classroom chairs in rows, similar to an airplane. Make sure there is an aisle. The rows can be numbered and the seats can have letters added. Row 1, Seats A, B, C, etc. Change the letters to match letters featured in your curriculum.

Airplane Travel *(cont.)*

Literacy Development *(cont.)*

- Serve snacks on board (using the stroller or shopping cart) while listening to an in-flight story or to music.

- Practice the poem below and note the rhyming words with the children.

Let's Fly!

When we want to fly up high,
Airplane tickets we can buy!

Make sure there is a tag
For every case and bag.

When luggage goes out of sight,
It is added to the flight.

Security, that's the rule,
Then the plane is filled with fuel.

Soon it will be time to go,
And our tickets we must show.

On the plane, now find a seat,
Store your bag, and have a treat.

Time for take off, here we go.
We'll be there before you know!

Variation for Younger Children

Board the plane,
It is time to go.

But first a ticket
You must show.

Numeracy Development

- Fill different suitcases with items in the classroom. Use newspaper, blocks, toys, a pillow, etc. Try to decide first by looking, then by lifting, which suitcase is the heaviest. Later, use a scale to weigh the luggage. Find the heaviest and the lightest suitcase. Line them up in order from heavy to light or vice versa.

- Set aside a box for measuring the size of carry-on luggage. Have each passenger try his or her piece of luggage. If the carry-on piece doesn't fit in the box, it will have to be tagged and checked!

- Number the boarding cards to match seat or row numbers on the plane. Seat numbers can be created using the number cards in the Appendix or on page 23.

- Have the captain count the passengers when they board and have the co-captain count the passengers as they deplane. Sort the boarding cards with children at the end of each dramatic play session.

- Have the flight attendants check their inventory at the beginning and end of each flight. Count out the number of beverage containers served per flight. Keep them in a numbered box for the next excursion.

- Scoop (measure) specific amounts of dry snack food (pretzels, trail mix, cereal, etc.) into the prepared waxed paper bags and staple them closed.

- Use the luggage carrier (wagon) to carry all the lunch boxes (or snacks) for a special luncheon picnic flight. Count the passengers and the food items. There should be a one-to-one ratio.

Airplane Travel *(cont.)*

Character Nametags

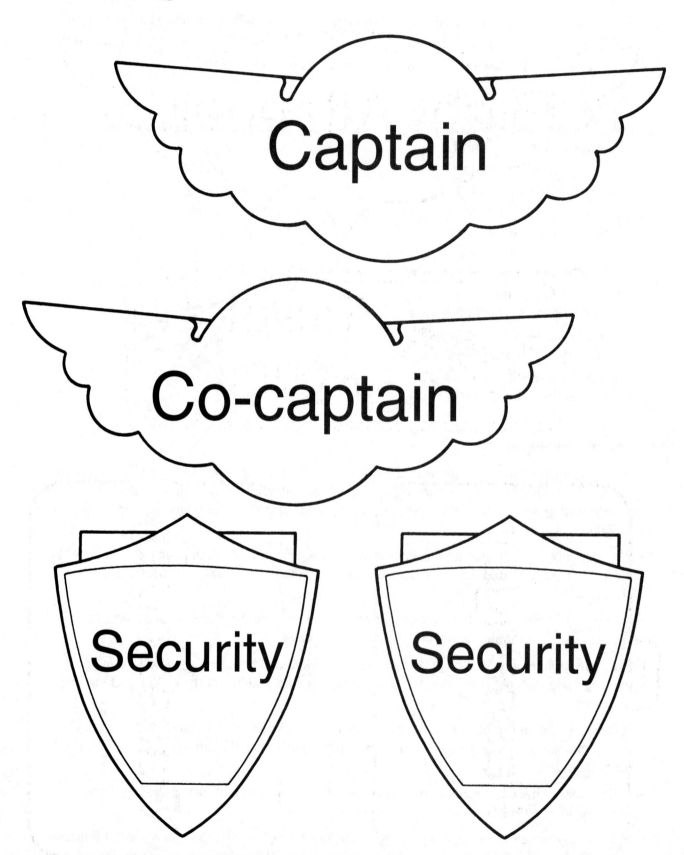

Airplane Travel (cont.)

Character Nametags (cont.)

Flight Attendant

Ticket Agent

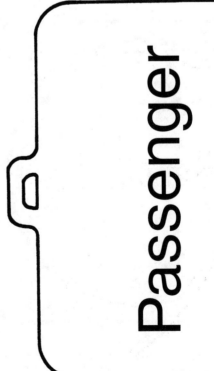

Passenger

Passenger

Airplane Travel *(cont.)*

Cockpit Gauges

Teacher Note: Enlarge, color, and cut out the patterns for the gauges. Attach them to a length of aluminum foil posted below the window in the cockpit.

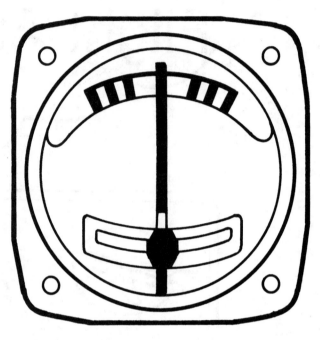

Airplane Travel *(cont.)*

Cockpit Gauges *(cont.)*

Teacher Note: Enlarge, color, and cut out the patterns for the gauges. Attach them to black or silver tagboard in the cockpit.

Airplane Travel *(cont.)*

Number each ticket to coordinate with a seat number. Color the tickets and laminate them. Copy the folder onto colored paper. Fold on the dashed line and staple or tape around the edges.

Seat Number

Ticket

Ticket Folder

Airplane Travel *(cont.)*

Boarding Passes

Boarding Pass for	Passenger	You have been assigned to sit in seat	

Seat Markers

A1	A2	A3
B1	B2	B3
C1	C2	C3
D1	D2	D3
E1	E2	E3
F1	F2	F3

Airplane Travel *(cont.)*

Captain's Hat

Copy the hat onto blue paper. Laminate the pattern and attach it to a paper band or to a wide strip of elastic.

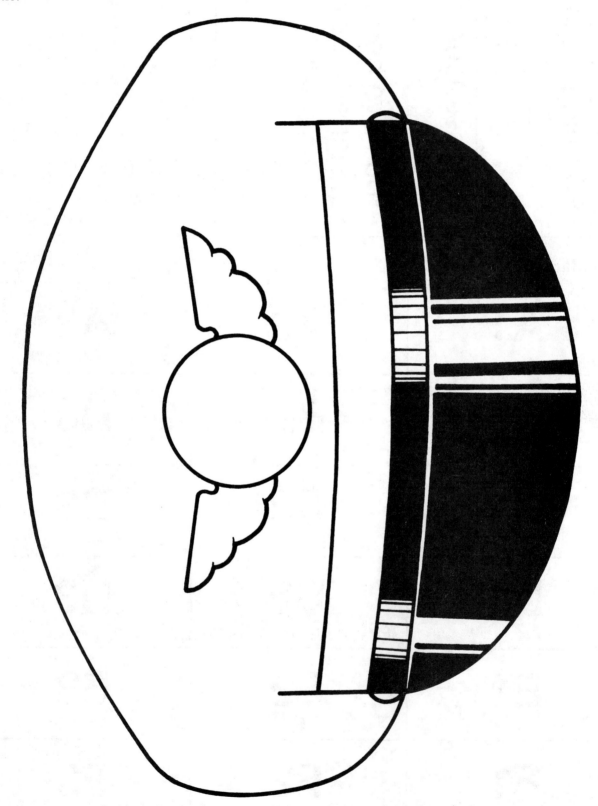

Safety Signs

No Smoking

Seatbelts On

Bakery

Lead Ins

- Present a variety of baked goods during group time. Choose four different items, such as a cookie, a cupcake, a cake, a scone, a muffin, a pie, or a croissant. Ask children to identify the items displayed. Have a taste test of the different items. (Be sure to check for children's allergies first.)

- Create a graph of different baked goods and ask children to take turns marking their favorite items on the graph. Afterwards, ask where you might find all these items on the same day. Discuss the options, including home, the local coffee shop, and the grocery store. Steer the discussion toward the theme—a bakery.

- Ask who has been to a bakery. Create a list of all the different things that one can purchase at a bakery. Add to the list as the literacy center develops.

- Show tools from a bakery, including cookie cutters and a whisk utensil. Consider playing a game where three or four items are displayed at a time and children identify the item that is not typically found in a bakery. For example, you might display a muffin tin, a cake pan, and a hammer. The children would identify the fact that a hammer would not typically be used in a bakery.

Bakery *(cont.)*

Suggested Materials for the Bakery

- aprons
- cans—all sizes
- bags and small bakery boxes
- baked goods patterns (page 34)
- birthday cake candles
- books about baking, recipes, and bakeries
- cake decorating tools
- cake decorations
- cake pans
- cake patterns (pages 32–33)
- cash register or money box
- children's books about bakeries, baking, or cooking
- coffee pot
- cookie cutters
- cookie sheets
- cups
- egg cartons and plastic eggs
- egg beater
- empty ingredient containers (flour, sugar, and spices)
- food magazines
- mixing bowls
- money (pages 246–247)
- pie pattern (page 35)
- pie plates
- baked goods (replicas)
- plates
- salt dough or clay
- rolling pins
- sifters
- spoons
- tea set
- wedding cake patterns (page 33)
- whisks
- wooden spoons

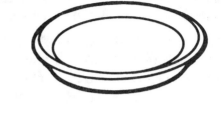

Safety Notes

Use tin, metal, plastic, or other unbreakable materials, rather than glass or ceramic.
Discuss safety around the stove and oven. Remind students that if they are going to bake at home they should let adults turn stoves and ovens on and off. Also, adults should be in charge of removing hot items from the oven or burners.

Bakery (cont.)

Teacher Preparation

1. Set up a counter area for the baked goods, a baking station with play dough to create baked goods, a cashier area with a money box or cash register, a notepad to write down orders, and a tip jar. If space allows, add a table for customers to enjoy their coffee, hot chocolate, and treats.

2. Make display cases for the food items. One way to make a display case for the counter area is to cut out a section of the bottom of one or two cardboard boxes that hold reams of paper. Tape clear acetate sheets to the cut out and stand the box on its side. The acetate "window" should be placed so that it faces the customers. The open space should face the person behind the counter so that he or she has access to the items.

3. Make labels for the bakery and nametags (page 31) for the participants. Additional labels for customers and a cashier can be found in the Appendix on page 256. Determine ahead of time how many bakers, customers, and counter persons will be in the bakery and make copies to suit.

4. Cut out and laminate pictures of baked goods. Prepare display trays with these items and any available plastic baked goods.

5. Arrange cups for coffee, tea, or hot chocolate.

6. Work with children to develop a list of items for sale or introduce the one on page 36. Determine prices for the price list and create the necessary money. See pages 246–247 in the Appendix for money reproducibles.

7. Demonstrate how to carefully place baked goods in bags or boxes for the customers.

8. Use the pie pattern to introduce the concept of fractions. Divide the pie into four equal slices. Discuss a whole pie, half a pie, and a quarter of a pie. (Make the connection between a quarter of a pie and a quarter of a dollar—four slices, four coins.)

9. Practice taking orders with the children. If appropriate, use the order sheet on page 36. Practice circling or checking the items ordered. Ahead of time, discuss whether or not more than one of each item can be ordered at a time. Instruct children to give the customer the order sheet when the order has been filled so that it can be double-checked.

10. Follow recipes to bake cookies. Have children cut out and decorate the cookies and sell them for a special snack. Do the same with bread recipes and sell them by the slice.

11. Bake and decorate a cake to commemorate a special event in the class. Avoid birthdays unless you can continue the cake making for each child throughout the year. Instead, use your imagination and find a group holiday or make up a special day (First Day of Winter, First Sprout in the Garden Day, Dinosaur Day, etc.)

12. Make a set of Wedding Cake Cans. Gather four or five cans of graduated sizes and cover them with white contact paper. Invite students to decorate them with wedding-related stickers and designs.

13. Create a counting activity for the children. Make a series of cakes using the patterns on pages 32–33. Have children decorate the cakes, laminate them, and program them with different numbers. Make paper birthday candles (or use real ones) and have children place the proper number of candles on each one.

14. If appropriate, visit a local bakery or baking area of a large grocery store or invite a local baker to be a guest speaker in your classroom.

28   ©Teacher Created Materials, Inc.

Bakery *(cont.)*

Student Preparation

1. Choose a name for the bakery and make a sign. Use a piece of paper shaped like a large, tiered wedding cake.

2. Cut out magazine pictures of baking ingredients (flour, butter, sugar, salt, spices, etc.). Cut out pictures of different baked goods or color and use the patterns on page 34. Make a collage for the bakery.

3. Cut out money, checkbooks, and credit cards (on pages 246–249) to use to purchase items in the bakery.

4. Fill the empty flour and sugar bags with sand, beans, or newspaper and tape them shut. Use them as props in the kitchen part of the bakery.

5. Practice writing dollar and cents signs. Use the reproducible on page 75.

6. Design wedding cakes using the patterns on page 33.

7. Use play dough to make different items for the bakery each day.

8. Fill in prices on the Bakery Price Lists.

Vocabulary Building

bake	dozen	raisins
bakery	half	rye
blend	knead	stir
bread	measure	temperature
cake	mix	tier
cold	muffin	tips
cool	nuts	warm
crimp	oven	wheat
croissant	pie	whole
cupcake	quarter	whole grain

Bakery *(cont.)*

Literacy Development

- Using play dough is a wonderful way to develop the fine motor skills needed to hold a writing implement. Use different colored play dough to create all kinds of treats while making little hands strong. Children can use a small rolling pin to roll out dough for cookie cutters. They can use their hands to shape snakes and coil them to create Danish or bear claw pastries. Dough can be kneaded to form cupcakes and muffins and crimped into pie tins for pies. Red or blue play dough can be used to make little fruit tarts.

- Follow the recipe on page 39 when making play dough to be used in the bakery or when baking items to be sold there. Read the directions aloud and have children repeat the steps as they are carried out.

- Use some of the words in the Vocabulary Building section to practice rhyming. Try making up silly poems with the rhyming words.

    bake—*break, cake, fake, lake, make, take, . . .*

    cold—*bold, fold, gold, hold, mold, sold, told, . . .*

    pie—*buy, die, guy, high, lie, my, rye, sky, tie, try, why, . . .*

- How many vocabulary words can be named that relate to temperature—cool, cold, hot, warm, boiling?

- Talk about which words used in the bakery are action words (verbs) and which are objects (nouns).

- Listening skills can be enhanced in the bakery by taking orders and serving the customers what they ordered. If children are old enough, these orders might involve ordering special cakes from the cake decorators as well.

- Have each child dictate a recipe to bake a bakery treat. Collect them and create a class Baker's Cookbook.

Numeracy Development

- A bakery is a great place to introduce the concept of "a dozen." Start with a 12-count egg carton and 12 eggs. Ask how many children know that 12 eggs in the carton are called a "dozen" eggs. How many eggs are in a half dozen?

- Make a dozen of each of the baked goods on page 34. Encourage students to sort and count the items. Note: Mini copies of the baked goods could be made that fit into egg cartons.

- Work with fractions. Talk about a whole pie, half a pie, and a quarter of a pie using the pie pattern on page 35.

- If appropriate, create addition and subtraction problems using the baked goods props or patterns.

Examples:

- If I have two muffins and one cupcake, how many baked goods do I have?

- If one cake costs $1.00, how much will two cakes cost?

- Practice stacking the Wedding Cake Cans. Place the largest can on the bottom and see how large a cake can be made.

- Discuss size. Use the Wedding Cake patterns to design wedding cakes, stacking the tiers from largest, on the bottom, to smallest, on the top.

Bakery (cont.)

Character Nametags

Baker

Counter Person

Cake Decorator

Bakery *(cont.)*

Cake Pattern

Place precut cake patterns in the bakery at each session. Invite the cake decorators to decorate the cakes using glue, glitter, glitter pens, felt pens, plastic flowers, ribbons, etc.

Note: The glue drying time will be similar to baking time and the cakes will not be ready for sale in the center until the following day.

Bakery *(cont.)*

Wedding Cake Patterns

Cut out the tiers of the wedding cake. Arrange the tiers on a sheet of construction paper. Place the largest tier on the bottom and work up to the smallest tier. If desired, cut out construction paper strips to form supports between the tiers.

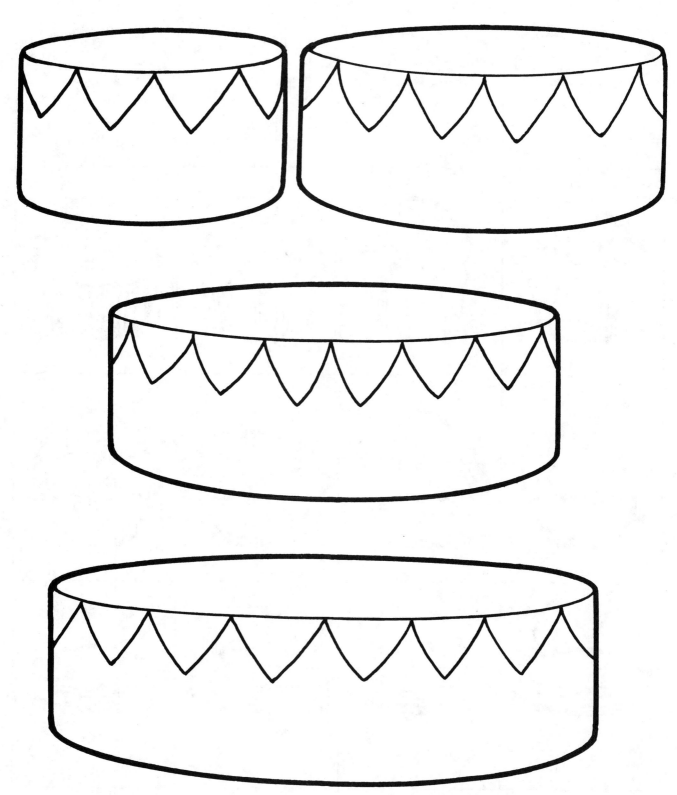

Bakery *(cont.)*

Baked Goods

Duplicate the pattern three times to create a dozen of each item. Color and cut out the baked goods.

Bakery *(cont.)*

Pie Pattern

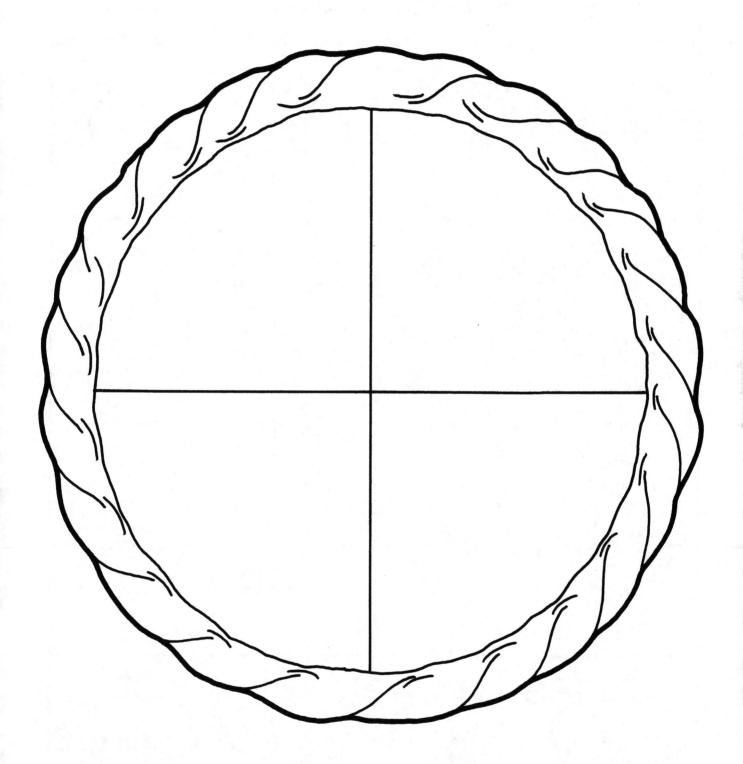

Bakery (cont.)

Order Sheet

Cookie		Lemon Bar	
Cupcake		Muffin	
Slice of Cake		Cake	
Slice of Pie		Pie	
Coffee	Tea		Hot Chocolate

Bakery (cont.)

Baked Goods Price List

Cookie		
Cupcake		
Muffin		
Scone		
Lemon Bar		
Slice of Pie		
Whole Pie		
Slice of Cake		
Whole Cake		

Beverage Price List

Coffee		
Tea		
Hot Chocolate		
Lemonade		
Juice		
Milk		

Bakery *(cont.)*

Play Dough Recipe

4 cups flour	2 cups salt
1.5 oz. (42 g) cream of tartar	4 cups water
4 tablespoons vegetable oil	food coloring (one small bottle)

Optional: liquid scent (lavender, almond, or orange)

1. Measure out the dry ingredients and mix them together in a large bowl.
2. Measure out the liquid ingredients—water, food coloring, and oil.
3. Combine the water, food coloring, and oil and bring them to a boil.
4. Combine the dry and liquid ingredients. Add the liquid scent. (The mixture will be hard to stir.)
5. Knead the dough when it has cooled.

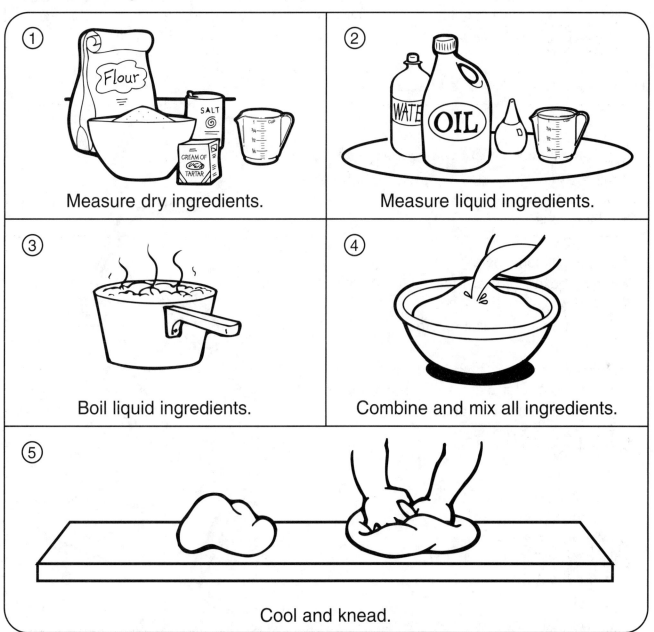

① Measure dry ingredients.

② Measure liquid ingredients.

③ Boil liquid ingredients.

④ Combine and mix all ingredients.

⑤ Cool and knead.

Doctor's Office

Lead Ins

- Hold up a stethoscope and ask what it is. Discuss the purpose of a stethoscope and ask where you might find one. Guide the discussion towards doctors and medical personnel and take a poll of who has been to a doctor's office. Do any of the children have parents in the medical profession?

- Discuss why people go to doctor's offices and what happens there. Talk about the different people who work in a doctor's office. Who helps the patients? Who helps the doctor? Ask children to describe the things used by each worker in the office. Mention tools, charts, and computers.

- Have a special whole-group discussion devoted to germs. Talk about ways we can protect ourselves and others from passing on germs that will make us sick. Stress the importance of hand washing and covering our mouths when we sneeze or cough. Consider having a cleaning day where each student gets to help clean up an area of the classroom. Introduce the hand washing signs. (page 114, Restaurant)

- Talk about why you would go to a pharmacy. Discuss why we take medicine and how we know what to take and when to take it. Reinforce that some medicines taste good or look like vitamins, but that they are not candies. Spend time discussing why it is important to never take medicine without permission.

Materials for the Doctor's Office

- bandages
- bedding
- children's books about visiting the doctor
- clipboards
- computers (old) and keyboards
- cotton balls
- crutches
- empty pill containers
- empty boxes for over-the-counter drugs and supplies
- eye chart
- file folders for medical records
- head sets
- hot water bottles
- lab coats or men's dress shirts (cut down)
- medicine containers (empty)
- nap mats or bedding
- notepads
- paper drapes
- scrubs (just the tops)
- stethoscope
- telephones
- tissues
- tongue depressors
- wheel chair
- x-rays (ask for old ones at a medical clinic or hospital)

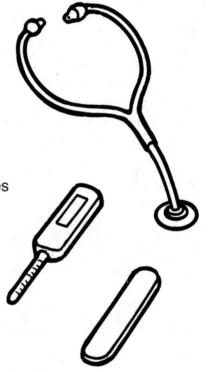

Doctor's Office (cont.)

Teacher Preparation

1. Set up the doctor's office. Arrange a check-in desk where patients can sign in for treatment. Arrange old computers and keyboards, telephones and headsets, charts and medical folders at a desk for the medical personnel.

2. Prepare a clipboard and some blank paper and pencils for a patient chart for the doctor or nurse to use.

3. Establish a sign-in area for patients. Use a clipboard or freestanding chart. Provide a chair or two in a "Waiting Room." Place age-appropriate books related to visiting a doctor's office next to the chairs.

4. Gather and arrange medical supplies—tissues, bandages, hot water bottles, bedding, tongue depressors, forehead fever strips, stethoscopes, paper gowns, etc. Create a checklist and containers for these items. Make sure the child who "closes" the office for the day counts the items as they are put away.

5. Decorate the office with posters illustrating the human skeleton or internal organs and medical supplies.

6. Make copies of the following items—the Human Body on pages 46 and 47, the Skeleton on page 48, and the Food Pyramid on page 49, and the Prescription Pads on page 50. Doctors and/or patients can refer to these as needed.

7. Enlarge the Skeleton (page 48) and the Human Body patterns (pages 46 and 47). Label them with children during a class discussion time prior to using the center.

8. Set up a separate pharmacy area if space allows. Stock the area with pill containers and empty boxes from medical supplies and over-the-counter medication. Determine a number of "pills" for each container and label it accordingly. Children can fill the pill containers with beans and practice counting the groups of beans in each container.

9. Create eye charts or use the one on page 52. If alphabet study is part of the curriculum, program a special eye chart with the letters being studied. Encourage children to identify the letters on the eye chart as part of their exams.

10. Assemble prescription pads (page 50). Determine how many pages will be on each pad and staple them together. Spend some time practicing with the completed prescription pads. Enlarge one page for demonstration purposes. Discuss the pictures (prescriptions). Explain what doctors do with the pads and why they are important. Use this opportunity to stress the importance of only taking medicine when a doctor or parent gives permission.

11. Display discarded x-rays in windows. Ask children to guess the skeletal part each x-ray depicts.

12. Invite a doctor, nurse, or other medical personnel to visit the classroom to share information about their jobs.

Teacher Note: Set up an adjoining hospital area if space allows. Lay a few nap mats down for patients to rest on. Have nurses attend to the patients while awaiting surgery. Doctors can schedule surgeries and other treatments. Visitors can come and go.

Safety Notes

Do not use thermometers or tools to examine ears for play. Explain to children that only adults with special training should use these tools. Instead, focus on pretending to set broken bones, bandage wounds, and perform "operations."

Doctor's Office *(cont.)*

Student Preparation

1. Make a large sign for the Doctor's Office. Write out the words in large letters on colorful paper and encourage the children to outline them or decorate them with bandages, cotton swabs, and tongue depressors.

2. Decorate boxes and containers for the doctor's supplies—cotton swabs, bandages, etc. Label each container. Make a chart showing how many of each item is in the office. Count them each day.

3. Review posters indicating body parts and organs.

4. Decorate an Open/Closed sign for the center. (page 245)

5. Review the labels and character nametags for the Doctor's Office and/or Hospital. Discuss costume options. Old white shirts, lab coats, scrub shirts, and stethoscopes should work well for most personnel.

6. Use old purses or shoeboxes to make doctor's bags. To make a doctor's bag, use the bottom part of a shoebox, a stapler or tape, black or brown construction paper and some cardboard. Cut out two cardboard handles. Center and staple the handles to the long sides of the shoebox. Press in the short sides of the box to make a fold. Press in the corners. Paint the box or cover the long sides with construction paper. Write *doctor* on the side.

Vocabulary Building

ache	germs	sneeze
appointment	headache	stethoscope
bandage	medicine	technician
Band-Aid®	needle	temperature
blood pressure cuff	nurse	thermometer
bones	pharmacy	tongue depressor
chart	prescription	vaccination
cough	scale	waiting room
doctor	scar	x-ray
earache	skeleton	

*Add body parts and organ names to the list

Doctor's Office (cont.)

Literacy Development

- Review the labels and the skeleton and body posters in the center. Name the body parts and label the enlarged posters.

- Discuss the doctor's chart. Mention how a doctor writes down what the patient says is bothering him or her. Encourage the "doctor" to write down what his or her "patient" describes.

- Explain the function of the prescription pads. Allow ample opportunities for children to use the charts, prescription pads, etc.

- Encourage "patients" and "medical personnel" to use the skeleton and body parts posters during their appointments. Patients can point to the body part or circle the area that is "hurt" or "aching."

- Spend some time discussing good nutrition using the food chart. Work these discussions into snack and lunch conversations. Consider making some labeled pictures of healthy foods that can be viewed during meal times. Hold up the picture and see who has that food item in his or her lunch. Spell the words together.

Numeracy Development

- Count body parts. Review the numbers 1, 2, 5, and 10 by discussing which body parts are one-of-a-kind (nose, mouth, heart, etc.), which come in pairs (hands, eyes, elbows, etc.), and which have five or ten similar parts (fingers and toes).

- Focus on the skeleton chart. How many bones can be counted in the leg, the arm, etc.? How many bones are in the human body? (206)

- Sort and count medical tools, tongue depressors, empty medicine bottles, etc. as a part of closing the Doctor's Office each day. Make sure the containers for these items are labeled appropriately. If appropriate, have children use the Supply List on page 51.

- When writing prescriptions, discuss how many days a patient should rest or stay off a broken foot, how many glasses of water he or she should drink, or how much medicine to take. Count out pill amounts for the prescription bottles in the pharmacy.

- Display a thermometer or a blood pressure cuff. Notice the numbers. Discuss the function of the numbers. Explain that the numbers on the instruments help determine whether someone is sick or not.

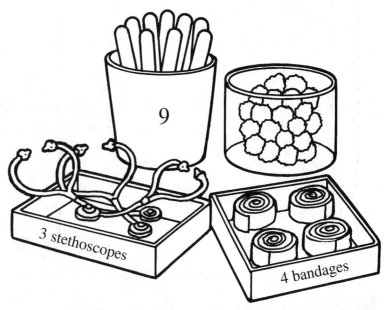

Doctor's Office (cont.)

Character Nametags

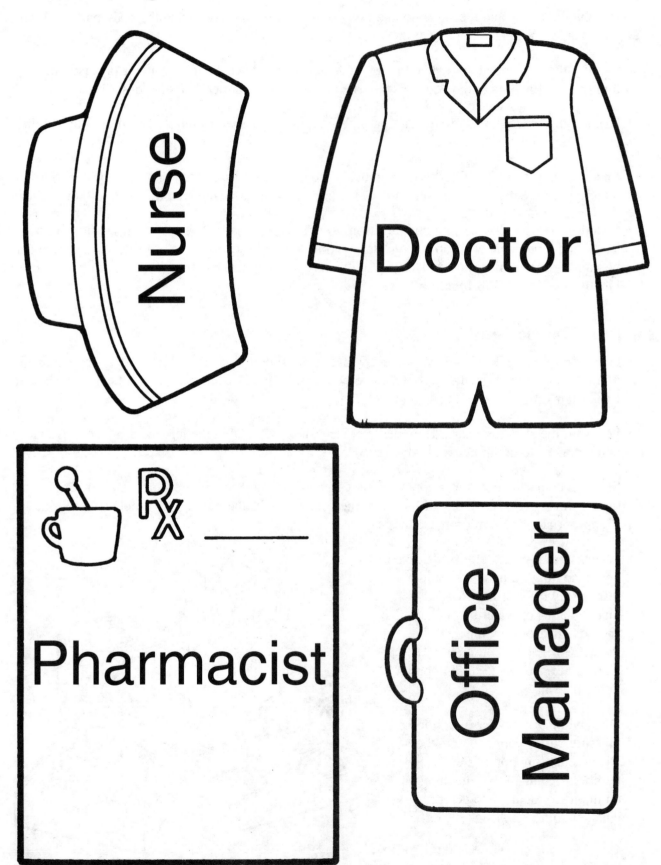

Nurse

Doctor

Pharmacist

℞ _____

Office Manager

Doctor's Office (cont.)

Character Nametags *(cont.)*

Patient

Patient

Patient

Patient

Doctor's Office *(cont.)*

Human Body

Exterior view

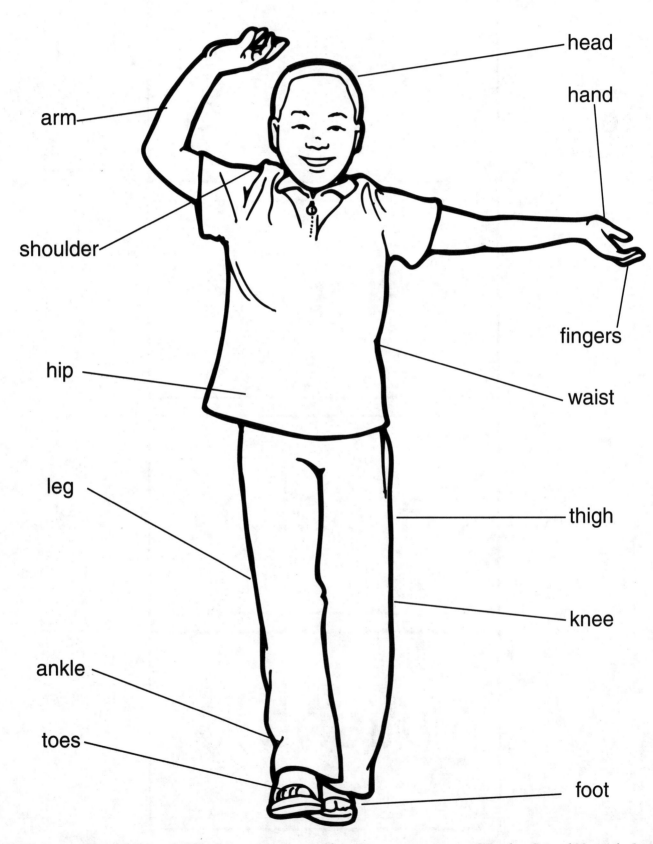

head

hand

arm

shoulder

fingers

hip

waist

leg

thigh

knee

ankle

toes

foot

Doctor's Office *(cont.)*

Human Body *(cont.)*
Interior view

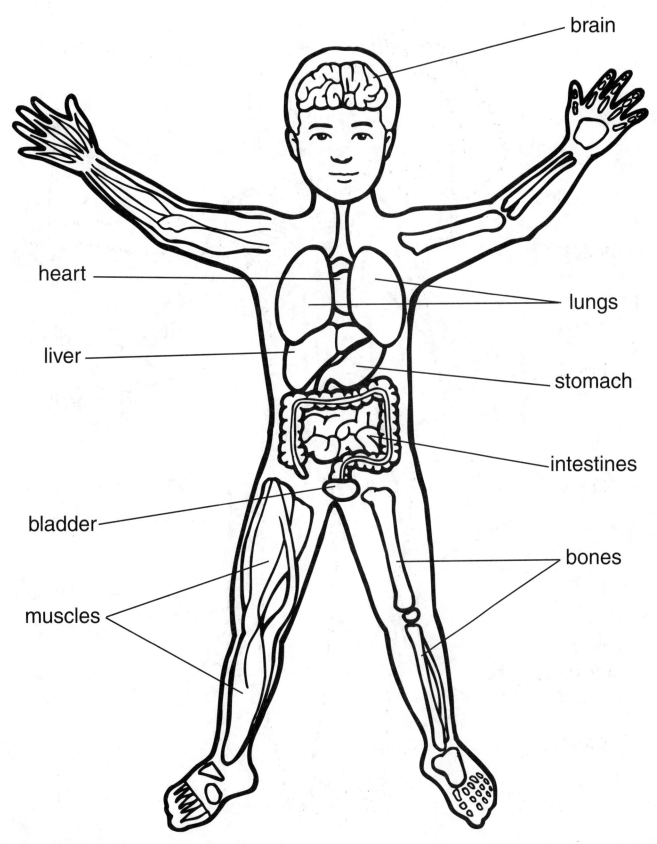

brain

heart

lungs

liver

stomach

intestines

bladder

bones

muscles

Doctor's Office *(cont.)*

Human Body *(cont.)*

Skeleton

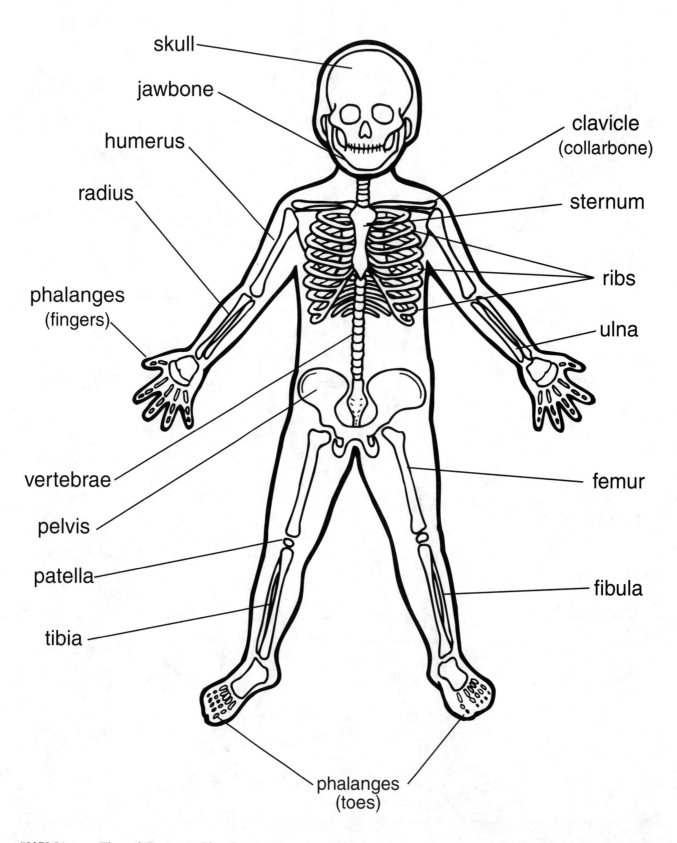

skull

jawbone

humerus

radius

phalanges
(fingers)

vertebrae

pelvis

patella

tibia

clavicle
(collarbone)

sternum

ribs

ulna

femur

fibula

phalanges
(toes)

Doctor's Office (cont.)

Food Pyramid

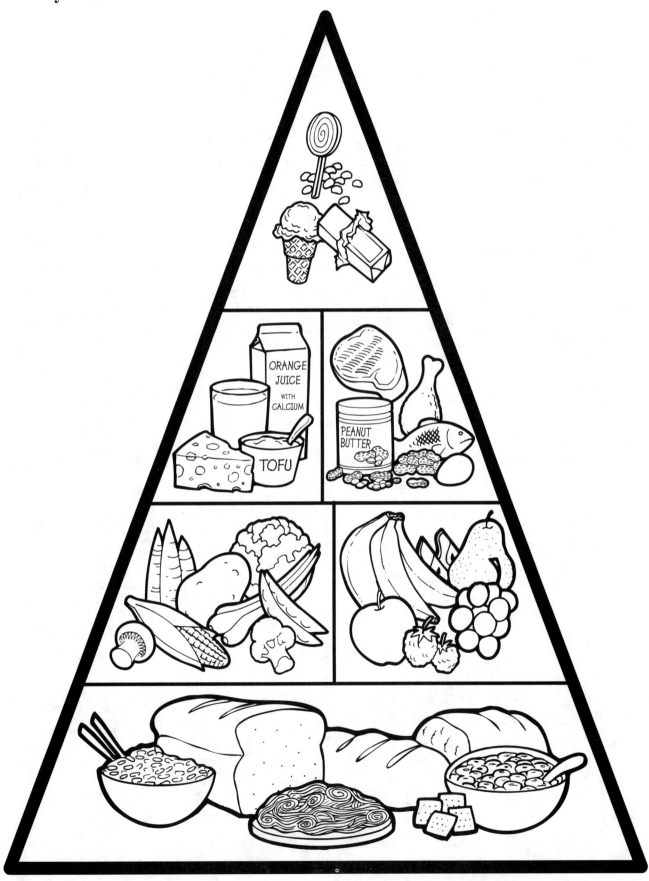

Doctor's Office *(cont.)*

Prescription Pad Pages

Doctor's Directions: Circle the treatment for your patient—rest, medicine, exercise, or operation.

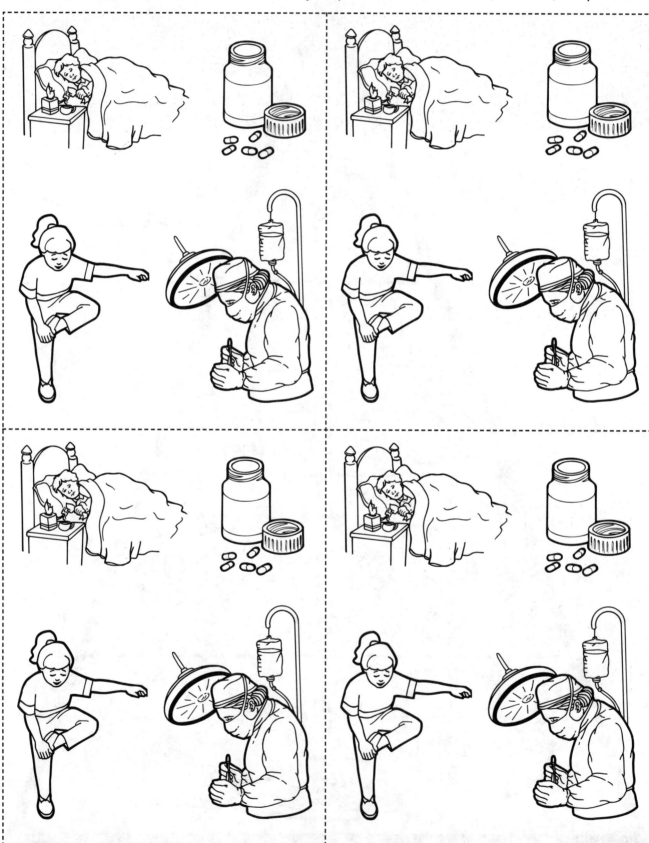

Doctor's Office (cont.)

Directions: Count the supplies in each container. Write the number of items in the box next to each supply.

Supply List			
Band-Aids®			
Bandages			
Stethoscopes			
Cotton Swabs			
Tongue Depressors			

Doctor's Office (cont.)

Eye Chart

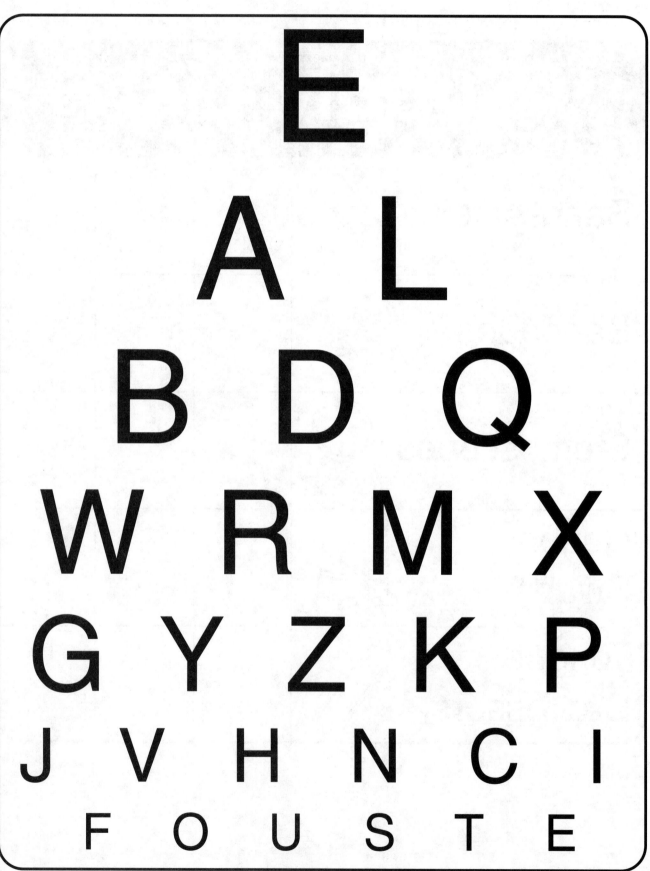

Flower Shop

Lead Ins

- Bring in a wrapped bouquet of flowers. Name the different flowers in the bouquet and talk about the wrapping. Ask where bouquets like the one you are holding are put together. Keep in mind that many large grocery stores have florist shops and that floral arrangements can also be purchased from street vendors. Focus on the type of florist shop in the area the children are familiar with and build on it.

- Demonstrate how to make floral arrangements. Show children how to place flowers in wreaths by weaving stems through the wires of a floral wreath. Show how to make centerpieces using Styrofoam. (See illustration.) The foam can be cut to fit a particular vase and covered with moss or pebbles after the flowers have been arranged. Place the centerpieces on the table during lunch and snack time, or give them as gifts to special people.

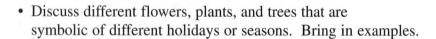

- Discuss why people receive flowers as gifts. Make a list of all the reasons you might give or receive flowers—birthdays, holidays, special party decorations, weddings. Share enlarged copies of the Arrangement Labels on page 60.

- Discuss different flowers, plants, and trees that are symbolic of different holidays or seasons. Bring in examples.

    Winter—*holly, poinsettias, wreaths, evergreens, trees, boughs*

    Spring—*tulips, daffodils, pussy willows, forsythia, cherry blossoms*

    Summer—*daisies, pansies, strawberries*

    Fall—*sunflowers, gourds, fall leaves*

- Discuss how different plants grow in different climates. Consider bringing in a small cactus and comparing it to a tulip or other flower indigenous to your area.

- Share a poster illustrating the parts of a flower (or use the picture on page 63). Discuss where flowers come from and allow the children to plant seeds. (Wheat grass seeds grow very quickly.)

- Demonstrate how to repot a plant. Draw attention to the roots, stems, and leaves. Examine different kinds of soil and potting mixes.

Hint: Set up the Flower Shop to coincide with Valentine's Day or Mother's Day. Celebrate the end of the center with a grand finale and present parents with bouquets of student-made flowers.

Flower Shop *(cont.)*

Suggested Materials for the Flower Shop

- baskets
- bins and containers to display flowers
- cash register or money box
- children's books about flowers, planting, and gardens
- computer and keyboards
- decorative pots
- delivery box, cart, or wagon
- floral decorations
- floral design magazines
- florist tape
- flower posters
- green floral foam
- money (pages 246–247)
- plastic flowers
- potted plants
- ribbons and bows
- seed catalogs
- seed packets
- silk flowers
- silk plants or trees
- spray bottles
- Styrofoam
- telephones
- tissue paper
- vases
- wagon
- watering cans
- wire wreath forms

Flower Shop (cont.)

Teacher Preparation

1. Set up a workspace for the bouquet preparation area. Include different sized pots, vases, flowers, wire wreath forms, Styrofoam blocks, florist tape, wire, etc., in the area. Try to have some large and small blocks of Styrofoam to fit in different sized pots or vases.

2. Demonstrate the arranging of flowers in vases and the use of wire forms and Styrofoam blocks. Encourage children to look in magazines to get ideas for different types of arrangements

3. Set up an area for customers to come in and place their orders. Place order pads, the computer and keyboard, the telephone, and other appropriate items in this area.

4. Make labels for the shop and nametags for the participants. Determine ahead of time how many children will arrange flowers, work the order counter, deliver flower arrangements, and play the parts of customers.

5. Determine a maximum number of participants and place a number card under the Flower Shop sign to remind students. Number cards can be found in the Appendix on page 242–244.

6. Make copies of the Price List on page 59 and the Arrangement Labels on page 60 if they will be used in the shop.

7. Make tissue-paper and construction-paper flowers for the shop (pages 64–66). Demonstrate how to make flowers with the students and keep additional supplies in the writing/craft area.

8. Determine prices for the products to be sold. Make the necessary make-believe money. (See Appendix pages 246–247.)

9. Have small cards available on the counter of the shop for children to attach to their flower arrangements. Keep a supply of cards, tissue paper, and colored paper in the writing/craft area for students to work with when the center is not available.

10. Discuss flower delivery and incorporate the service in the shop. Establish the way the flowers will be transported. Will the delivery person carry them, put them in a wagon, or push a special box along the floor?

Flower Delivery

11. Create pattern strips using the flower patterns on page 62 for children to copy or color.

12. Plan a visit to a local florist shop, nursery, or special neighborhood garden.

Flower Shop *(cont.)*

Student Preparation

1. Determine a name for the florist shop and make a sign for it. Decorate the border of the sign with cutout leaves and flowers. Use the patterns on pages 61–62.

2. Make flowers using the patterns on pages 61–62 or design your own.

3. Use pictures from seed catalogs and floral magazines to create a mural or to make posters for the shop. Make a sign for the delivery vehicle.

4. Decorate copies of the Arrangement Labels on page 60. Use the labels when designing arrangements.

5. Create a garden outside or on a windowsill. Plant and care for flower seeds and seedlings. Offer to take over the watering of shrubs and trees on site.

6. Practice tying bows. (It is just like tying shoes.) Wrap floral arrangements in colored tissue paper and tie bows around them.

7. Convert a box, a cart, or wagon into a delivery car. Use the vehicle to deliver finished arrangements to specific people or locations. (See illustration.)

8. Prepare the checkbooks, money, and credit cards needed to purchase flowers and plants at the shop.

9. Decorate an Open/Closed sign (Appendix, page 245) with flower stickers and display it at the entrance of the dramatic play center.

Vocabulary Building

arrange	dozen	pot
arrangement	floral	roots
bouquet	flower	stem
centerpiece	leaf	tree
delivery	leaves	vase
design	plant	wreath

Note: Add flower names particular to the flower shop that has been created.

Flower Shop *(cont.)*

Literacy Component

- Have the children make signs, price sheets, and price tags for the flower shop. They can practice taking orders and writing them down.

- Enhance listening skills in the flower shop by taking orders and arranging the type, size, and color of flowers ordered by each customer.

- Make floral arrangements to match the price lists.

- Spend time reviewing the signs and labels posted around the room. Encourage children to add more as they think of them.

- Encourage children to paint or draw flower pictures at an easel. Developing shoulder, wrist, and hand coordination will facilitate the fine-motor coordination necessary to hold writing implements.

- Create a matching game of different flower pictures. Use seed packets or make two copies of the six flower patterns on page 62. Color the matching flowers the same color. Laminate the cards and use them to play a memory game where the cards are placed facedown and students, in turn, flip over two cards, trying to make a match. Make additional sets for patterning activities.

- Have children dictate message cards to accompany their flower arrangements. Help them sign the cards.

Numeracy Component

- All shops offer opportunities to learn about money and the flower shop is no different. Offer opportunities for "customers" to pay using money (pages 246–247), writing checks (page 249) and signing credit cards (page 248).

- Have children count out the flowers used in each arrangement.

- Discuss the concepts of a half dozen (6) and a dozen (12). Order a dozen flowers of one color or order a dozen made up of a specific number of flowers (i.e., three red flowers, three blue flowers, three white flowers, and three yellow flowers).

- Sort and count the flowers in the store by color. Make tally or graphing sheets or use the ones on page 67 to keep track of how many of each flower were counted.

- Practice taking orders over the phone for flowers and writing down how many flowers the callers want.

- Use the Life Cycle of a Flower cards on page 220 to practice sequencing and ordinal numbers—*first, second, third, fourth.*

Flower Shop *(cont.)*

Character Nametags

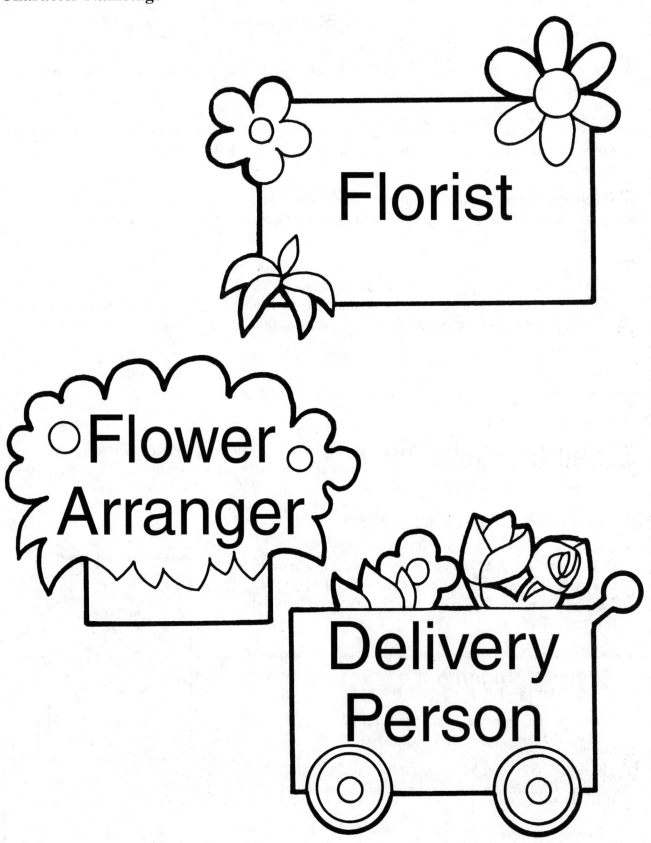

Flower Shop *(cont.)*

Price List

Flower		
A Dozen Flowers	**12**	
Small Bouquet		
Large Bouquet		

Small Arrangement	Large Arrangement

Flower Shop *(cont.)*

Arrangement Labels

 Happy Birthday

 **Best Wishes on Your Wedding**

 **Get Well Soon**

 Welcome Home

 **Happy Graduation**

 **A New Baby**

Flower Shop *(cont.)*

Copy onto different shades of green construction paper. Cut out the leaf patterns.

Leaf Patterns

Flower Shop *(cont.)*

Color and cut out the flower patterns. Attach finished flowers to pipe cleaners using tape. Add leaves.

Flower Patterns

tulip

daisy

rose

carnation

daffodil

violet

Flower Shop (cont.)

Parts of a Flower

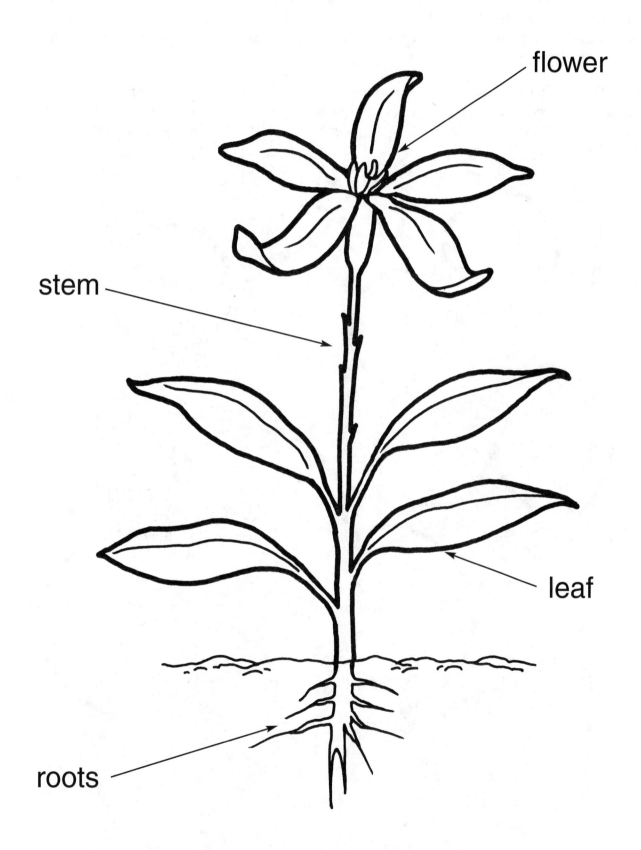

flower

stem

leaf

roots

Flower Shop *(cont.)*

Construction-Paper Flowers

Directions for the Teacher: Make multiple copies of these patterns on different colored sheets of construction paper. Divide the patterns into three groups—flower centers (circles), small petals, and large petals. Each group should have a variety of color choices.

Directions for the Flower Designer: For each flower, cut out a large flower petal shape, a small flower petal shape, and a center. Try to use three different colors. Glue the center to the middle of the small petal shape and then glue the small petal onto the larger petal. Tape or glue a pipe cleaner to the back for a stem.

Flower Shop *(cont.)*

Tissue Paper Flowers

Directions: For large flowers, cut different-colored tissue paper into 8" (20 cm) x 18" (46 cm) strips. Use two or three strips per flower.

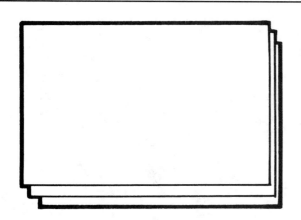

1. Lay the strips on top of each other.

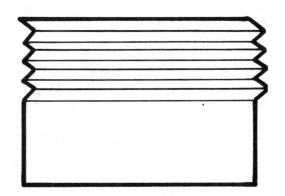

2. Fold the strips back and forth as if you were making a fan.

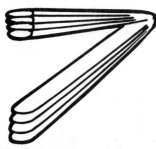

3. Bend the folded strips in half to make a crease mark. Use scissors to make rounded or pointed edges on the end opposite the crease.

4. Open the fold and twist a pipe cleaner or a rubber band around it. That will become the center of the flower.

5. Fan out the tissue on either side of the pipe cleaner (or band).

6. Hold the flower at the pipe-cleaner twist or by hooking one finger into the rubber band. Separate the layers of tissue and pull them toward the center.

Flower Shop *(cont.)*

Paper Strip Flowers

Materials (per flower)
- construction paper— two different colors
- glue stick
- green pipe cleaner

Directions

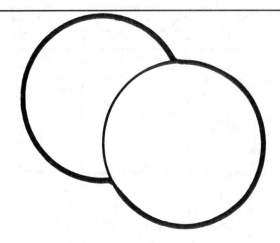

1. Cut two circles approximately 3½"/9 cm from one color construction paper.

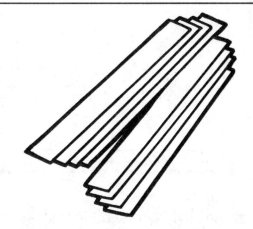

2. Cut 8 strips approximately 1" x 4½"/ (2.5 cm x 11.5 cm) from a second color construction paper.

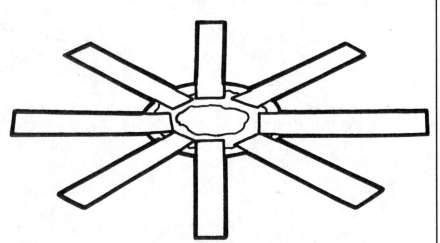

3. To assemble the flower, lay one of the circles on a flat surface and cover it with glue, using a glue stick. Arrange the strips around the circle so that approximately ¼" (.6 cm) of each strip is attached to the glue.
Lay the end of a green pipe cleaner on the circle as well.

4. Cover the tops of the attached strips with more glue and fold the strips over to form loops.

5. Cover the assembly with the second circle and allow time to dry. **Optional:** Add seeds to the center.

Flower Shop *(cont.)*

Color Tally Sheet

Red			
Yellow			
Blue			
Pink			
Purple			
White			

Grocery Store

Lead Ins

- Bring a bag of grocery props to discuss and ask children in what kind of store the items in the bag can be purchased. Note the different words children use—grocery store, market, store, supermarket. Make a list of the different names. Ask the children to name the grocery stores in their area.

- Discuss where grocery store food originates. Mention farms, gardens, orchards, the ocean, factories, and canneries. Remind children that some foods, like fruits and vegetables, come straight from the fields. Others, like fish, come from the ocean. Still others, like tuna fish, come from the ocean and then need to be processed at a cannery. Grains used in cereals come from farms (fields) and then go to factories to be turned into cereal. This can be an ongoing discussion with the children. Periodically discuss the origins of different snack foods or lunch items. As students become adept at this activity, show or share pictures of new or different foods.

- How does the food get to the store? Mention the big delivery trucks that bring products to the store. Discuss the different jobs people who work in a grocery store do each day. Graph each child's choice of a job in a grocery store. Include manager, checker, stock person, and bagger. Add other jobs particular to a store in the area, such as a produce clerk, a florist, or a butcher.

- Introduce the idea of a checkout stand. Talk about the different types of food carriers in a store. Discuss baskets, carts and other options.

- Discuss the way people pay for groceries in a grocery store. Discuss the scanner. Teach children how to find the scanning code on each product in the store.

- Demonstrate how to use the checkout stand made for the classroom. (See page 70, Teacher Preparation, step 4.) Practice sliding items along the black paper.

- Discuss the bagger's important job. Mention that he or she has to be careful when packing up fragile items. Add that a bagger needs to make sure that he or she does not make the bags too heavy to carry.

Grocery Store (cont.)

Suggested Materials for the Grocery Store

- adding machine tape
- aprons
- baseball caps or hats
- cash register or money box
- children's books about grocery stores and grocery products
- coupon pages from newspapers and magazines
- dress-up clothes, purses, and wallets for shoppers
- empty boxes—pasta, cereal, aluminum foil, detergent, etc.
- empty cans with labels
- food magazines
- grocery advertisements
- labels (to write prices on)
- meat trays
- mini shopping carts
- money (pages 246–247)
- oatmeal containers
- old newspapers
- paper shopping bags (small and large)
- plastic fruit, vegetables, and other food items
- sack of beans
- scales
- shopping baskets
- silk or plastic flowers
- strawberry baskets

Safety Note: Do not use plastic grocery bags with young children; use paper bags instead.

Grocery Store (cont.)

Teacher Preparation

1. Set up shelves or counters to display the products to be sold. If possible, create and number different aisles within the store. Consider having separate sections for produce, a bakery, meats, canned goods, cereal, etc., depending on the materials at hand. If plastic fruits and vegetables are available, arrange them in baskets. Have a scale handy for weighing the produce. Place food items in a deli case. (Convert the display case from the bakery, page 28, to create a deli case.)

2. Fill the empty boxes with beans, newspaper, or other packing materials. This will help them stand more easily on the shelves and will help the boxes endure repeated sales and bagging. Tape the filled boxes closed. Add appropriate prices. Stock the store shelves. **Note:** Before officially stocking the shelves, share the products with the children. Determine what section of the store they think each item should be placed. Make certain each section has a sign.

3. Display the posters and signs made by the children in the appropriate locations. Mark certain items "on sale." Make sure that every item has a price tag. If appropriate, encourage the children to write the prices on the labels.

4. Create a checkout stand for the checker. A small table will work. Place the cash register in the center. Have a roll of adding machine tape next to the cash register so that the checker can tear off receipts for the customer. Line the table with two or three sheets of black construction paper to simulate the check out conveyer belt/scanner. Stock paper grocery bags and lunch bags at the end where the bagger will stand.

5. Make labels for the store and nametags for the participants. Determine ahead of time the number of checkers, managers, shoppers, and baggers your store can accommodate and make nametags to suit. Determine a maximum number of participants and place a number card under the grocery store sign to remind students. Number cards can be found in the appendix on pages 242–244.

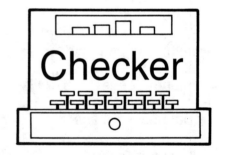

6. Make vests (page 251) and/or aprons (page 252) to go with the character nametags. Use baseball caps or hats for some employees.

7. Pretend the store is offering taste tests of certain snacks. Place the snacks on trays at the end of one of the store aisles. Have the store personnel serve the snack to customers.

8. Glue pictures of different products to index cards to be used in a guessing game. Laminate the cards. Children can take turns selecting a card and giving hints about it.

9. Schedule a trip to a local grocery store or invite someone from the store to come to the classroom.

Grocery Store (cont.)

Student Preparation

1. Make a sign for the grocery store. Decorate the sign with coupons and grocery store receipts. Make additional signs for the other departments in the store.

2. Collect pictures of food from magazines, food advertisements, and newspapers. Cut out pictures of fruits and vegetables to put on a sign for the produce area. Use pictures of meat for the sign for the meat department or butcher. Sandwiches, salads, and fried chicken pictures could be used on the deli sign. Use the rest of the cut-out pictures to make food posters in different sections of the store.

3. Put plastic fruits and vegetables in plastic or cardboard strawberry baskets. Arrange them in the store under the produce sign.

4. Arrange plastic foods in meat trays for the deli section of the grocery store.

5. Help the teacher stuff the boxes and bags that will be used on the store shelves. Measure out a cup or two of beans for each box. Fill the rest with newspaper and tape the boxes closed.

Vocabulary Building

aisle	discount	produce
bagger	display	sale
butcher	dollar	sale item
cashier	florist	sample
cents	frozen	scanner
charge	groceries	taste test
checker	half off	two-for-one
day-old	perishable	
deli	price tag	

Grocery Store *(cont.)*

Literacy Component

- Collect items from the store and sort them in different ways. Sort food items and household items. Sort foods in terms of breakfast, lunch, dinner, and snack. Sort by the type of packaging. Does the item come in a box, a bag, or other type of container?

- Incorporate size and shape words when describing products. (Example: A box of detergent is *large*, *square*, and *heavy*.)

- Use adjectives to describe an item in the store. Ask the children to guess what item is being described. (Example: I am thinking of something that comes in a box. You pour it into a bowl and add milk to it.) After a few tries, divide the class into pairs and have them play the game together.

- Discuss the word *fragile*. Discuss the items in a store that are fragile—eggs, avocados, items in glass jars, etc. Start a list and keep adding to it. Discuss the word *perishable* and create a second list of related items. As the center draws to a close, combine the two lists to create a Venn diagram. Which items are fragile, perishable, or both fragile and perishable?

- For younger children, supply paper for them to write lists in their own way. This may be scribbling or a series of alphabet letters. Encourage the children to copy words from the products when writing their shopping lists.

- Make a chart about where certain foods originate. Headings might include *Farm, Ocean, Factory, Cannery,* and *Bakery*. Remind children that some foods, like fruits and vegetables, come straight from the fields. Others, like fish, come from the ocean. Still others like tuna fish, come from the ocean and then need to be processed at a cannery. Grains used in cereals come from farms (fields) and then go to factories to be turned into cereal. Have children cut out pictures of different foods and place them in the appropriate column on the chart. Stress that grocery products come to the store from many different places, which makes it convenient for us.

Numeracy Component

- Determine prices for each item in the store. Have children affix prices to the products in the store. Change prices occasionally to reflect sales and to introduce new numbers.

- Compare prices. Find the most expensive and the least expensive item sold in the grocery store. Find items that are the same price.

- Use the scales in the produce department to weigh different items. Find the heaviest and the lightest items. Find items that weigh the same. Compare the weights of plastic foods and their real counterparts. (Example: Which weighs more, a plastic apple or a real apple?)

- Arrange items in the store by size, from largest to smallest and vice versa. Find products that are the same size. Try *tall* to *short* and *thick* to *thin*.

- Practice bagging a stack of groceries. Divide the weight evenly between two bags. See how many objects can fit into a bag. Remember to put the fragile items on top.

Grocery Store (cont.)

Character Nametags

Grocery Store *(cont.)*

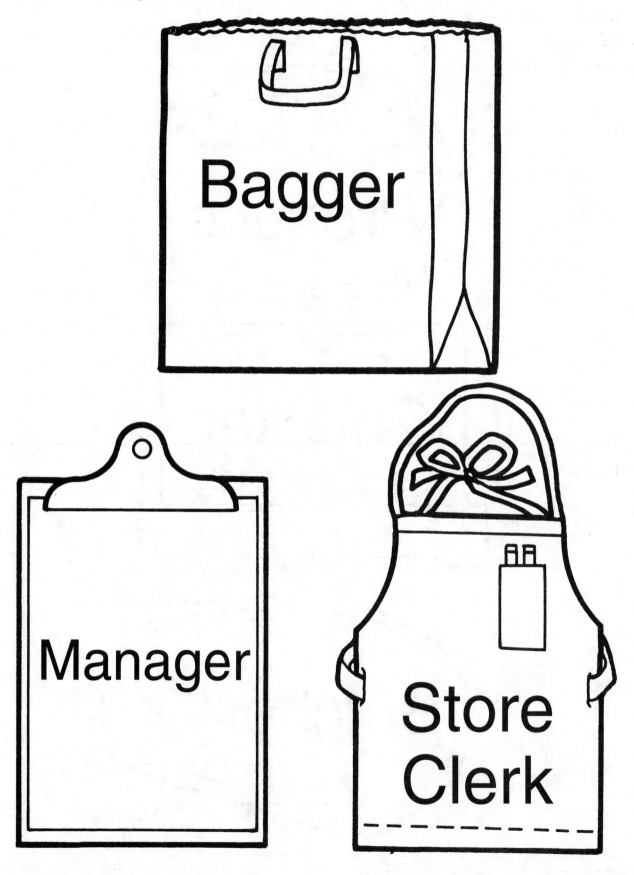

Grocery Store *(cont.)*

Money Symbols

Directions: Trace the symbols and the words.

Dollar Sign

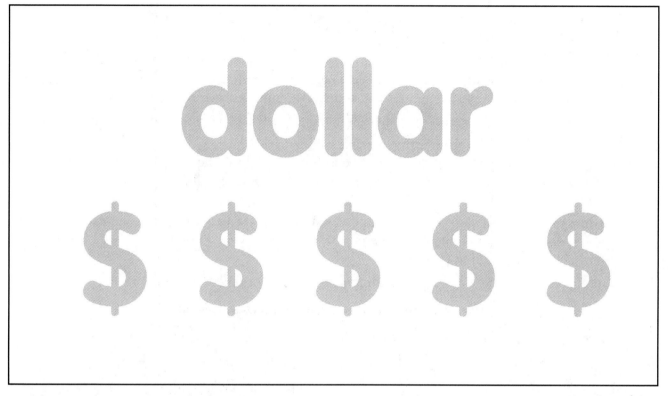

Cent Sign

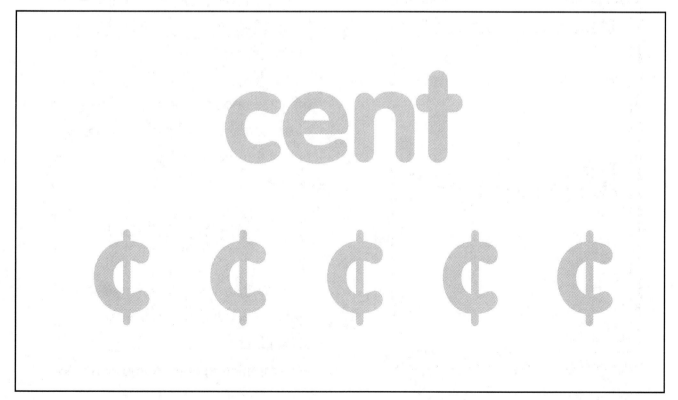

Pet Store

Lead Ins

- Bring in a pet for a day and share it with the children. Discuss the pet's diet, sleep patterns, and exercise needs. Ask where the animal might have come from. Guide the children to the idea of a pet store.

- Poll the children to see who has pets and what kinds of pets they own. Make a list of all the pets in the class and graph the responses.

- Bring in pictures of different domestic and wild animals and display them for the children. Discuss where each animal lives. Sort the animals into two groups—domestic and wild. Explain that the next center will be about domestic animals or animals that can live safely in our homes.

- Discuss endangered species and explain how some animals are becoming so rare that they are protected and can no longer be kept as pets.

- Put samples of three or four types of pet food on display and ask the children which pets might eat each food. Try birdseed (birds), live crickets (spiders and some lizards), lettuce (iguanas and turtles), and dog biscuits (dogs).

- Consider introducing a class pet at this time. First, discuss the pet, its habitat, and its needs. Establish a schedule for caring for the animal. Share books about proper care of the animal. Vote on a name and make a sign for the pet.

Safety Note: Check for allergies before bringing animals, hay, or other pet-related materials into the classroom.

Suggested Materials for the Pet Store

- animal magazines
- animal posters
- baskets (large)
- bird cages
- bird seed
- bowls for animal food
- boxes
- cages
- cash register or money box
- cat carriers
- cat litter
- children's books related to pets and pet stores
- crickets
- dog and cat collars
- dog biscuits
- dog leashes

- empty cans and bags of pet food
- empty containers of pet care products
- fish bowls
- fish tanks
- measuring tape
- money (pages 246–247)
- pet care books
- plastic animals (pet store variety)
- pet picture cards (pages 81–82)
- pillows
- rulers
- scales
- scoopers
- sequins, glitter, and small plastic jewels
- stuffed animals (pet store variety)
- terrariums
- water bottles (for tanks and habitats)

Pet Store *(cont.)*

Teacher Preparation

1. Gather all the stuffed or plastic animals that have been collected and place them in appropriate homes. Ask the children to create or decorate some of these homes. Place birds in bird cages, fish in fish bowls, lizards and snakes in terrarium tanks, etc. Place pillows in baskets to create dog and cat beds. Incorporate live pets, such as the class hamster, if appropriate. Unusual animals can be marked with special signs (page 83) that say "Not for Sale" or "Handle with Care."

2. Arrange the different habitats in the pet store. Make sure there are food dishes and water containers in each one. If cages are not available, create them using different-sized boxes. Cut openings or bars in the boxes to suit the needs of the "pets."

3. Make labels for the store areas and for the different animals for sale. Laminate nametags for the participants. (See page 80 and the Appendix for additional nametags.) Determine ahead of time the number of sales people, owners, customers, etc., your Pet Store can accommodate and make copies to suit. Review labels with the children.

4. Determine a maximum number of participants and place a number card under the Pet Store sign to remind students. Number the pets in each habitat as well. The numbers for the animals can be adjusted as sales are made. Number cards can be found in the appendix on pages 242–244.

5. Gather or create uniform items to go with the character nametags.

6. Arrange a display area for books about pets and pet care. Place empty containers of pet care products, food, leashes, and collars nearby.

7. Create a cashier area and a price sheet for the store based on the inventory. Have adding machine tape available so the cashiers can give receipts. Make or have children make the necessary make-believe money.

8. Set up a schedule for children to take turns bringing their pets in for a day to share. Have them discuss the responsibilities of taking care of pets. What is fed to the animal? How often is the pet fed? Does the animal need to be walked? How does the animal bathe? Who picks up after the animal?

9. Use an old plastic baby tub to create a dog grooming area. Add some towels, but explain that the water is pretend.

10. Create a doghouse out of a large box. Let the children take turns playing in the doghouse.

11. Enlarge and color the pictures on pages 81–82. Laminate the pictures and the labels. Use them as labeling activities in a center or during group times.

12. Arrange a visit to a pet store, a veterinary clinic, or the Humane Society or have a guest speaker come into the classroom.

Pet Store *(cont.)*

Student Preparation

1. Vote on a name for the pet store and make a sign. Decorate the sign with dog and cat treats. For added fun, make the sign on a large sheet of paper shaped like a fish or a dog bone.

2. Decide on prices for the different animals for sale and make price tags. Attach the price tags to each animal's habitat.

3. Make animal carriers using boxes. Make sure the "pet" will fit comfortably into the size box chosen. Get help cutting openings in the box. Make at least one window and one door. Decorate the boxes with pictures of the animal, descriptive words, or pictures of food and toys the animal might use.

4. Cut out pictures of different kinds of pets. Sort them and use them to decorate posters for each section of the pet store (birds, dogs, cats, snakes, etc.).

5. Design cat, dog, and fish food labels. Glue the labels onto cans. Arrange the cans in a section of the store.

6. Make dog and cat collars for the "pets" using tag board or felt strips. Wrap the strip around the animal's neck and allow for a little overlap. Cut the strips to the appropriate lengths and decorate them with felt pens, sequins, small plastic jewels, glitter, etc.

7. Decorate an Open/Closed sign for the pet store. Display it at the entrance of the store.

Vocabulary Building

bird	gerbil	pet
cat	hamster	puppy
chinchilla	hermit crab	rabbit
dog	iguana	reptile
fish	kitten	snake
frog	lizard	spider
gecko	mammal	wild

Enrichment Words

amphibian	domestic	grooming
diurnal	endangered	nocturnal

Pet Store (cont.)

Literacy Component

- Make a list of all the pets the children have. Create a graph based on the list. Include pictures of the pets and word labels. Encourage the children to bring in pictures of their pets.

- Ask the children to name different breeds of dogs, cats, or birds. Make lists and add names and pictures to them often.

- Have the children dictate stories about the pets they have or wish they could have. Help them use descriptive words. Have each child illustrate his or her story. Make copies of the illustrated stories and bind them together for a class book. Display the book in the pet store.

- Learn the adult and baby names for different animals—rabbit/kit or kitten, dog/puppy, cat/kitten, horse/pony, cow/calf, etc. Start a list and keep it going for the duration of the center. Quiz each other.

- Create a matching game using the word and picture cards on pages 81–82. Color and laminate the cards. Make a corresponding set of word cards to match the animals chosen. **Hint:** Place the name of the animal on the back of the picture card so the children can check their work.

- Use the cards on pages 84–86 to do labeling activities. Cut out the cards and the place the labels in the appropriate places. Some word cards, like fur, feathers, and scales can be placed anywhere on the body. Create new picture cards and labels as time allows.

- Discuss the difference between the word *dangerous* and the word *endangered*.

- Use the labeling cards on pages 84–86 to learn or review the body part names of different animals.

Numeracy Component

- All of the lists, charts, and graphs created for the pet store will enhance children's numeracy and literacy skills. Encourage children to add to these lists and recount the totals on a regular basis.

- Create a chart with the names and pictures of animals in the store. If it is not possible to take pictures of the animals in the store, have the children draw pictures. Beside each picture, put an X or a check mark for each animal of that kind in the store. Update the chart as animals arrive or are "sold." Each time the chart is viewed, count out the number of checks or X's in each row. Write that number at the end of the row or place the appropriate number card beside it.

- Determine the two most common pets owned by students in the class. Create a Venn diagram for these two pets. Have each child place his or her name in the appropriate section of the diagram. (If children are not yet comfortable writing their names, give them each a small sticky note to place in the appropriate section.) Use the center of the diagram for children who have both featured pets. Let children who have neither pet choose which pet they wish they had. Count the totals in each section and post the results.

- Count and compare animals. Divide the pets in the store into groups based on the number of feet they have.

- Weigh and measure the animals, their food, and their homes.

Pet Store *(cont.)*

Character Nametags

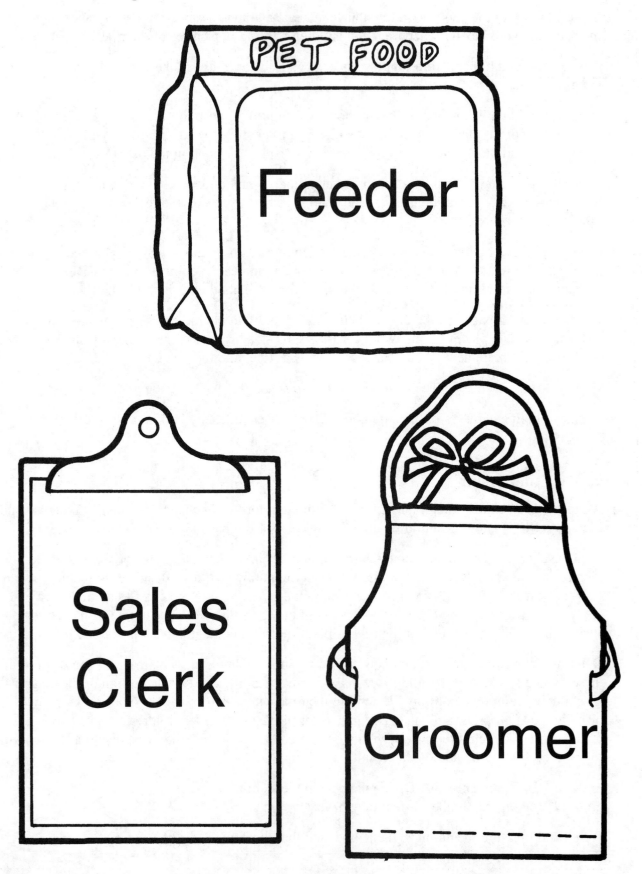

Feeder

Sales Clerk

Groomer

Pet Store *(cont.)*

Pet Picture Cards

Color and cut out the pictures below and on page 82. Cut out the coordinating labels. Glue the pictures to colored construction paper. Glue one set of labels on the back of each picture. Make a matching set of cards with the animal name labels on them. Laminate all the cards.

bird   dog

rabbit   fish

cat   frog

Pet Store (cont.)

Pet Picture Cards (cont.)

Color and cut out the pictures below and on page 81. Cut out the coordinating labels. Glue the pictures to colored construction paper. Glue one set of labels on the back of each picture. Make a matching set of cards with the animal name labels on them. Laminate all the cards.

hamster	kitten
lizard	puppy
snake	mouse

Pet Store Signs

Not for Sale

Handle with Care

Pet Store *(cont.)*

Labeling

bird

beak	feet	wing
feathers	tail	head

Pet Store (cont.)

Labeling (cont.)

cat

ears	tail	whiskers
fur	paws	claws

Labeling *(cont.)*

fish

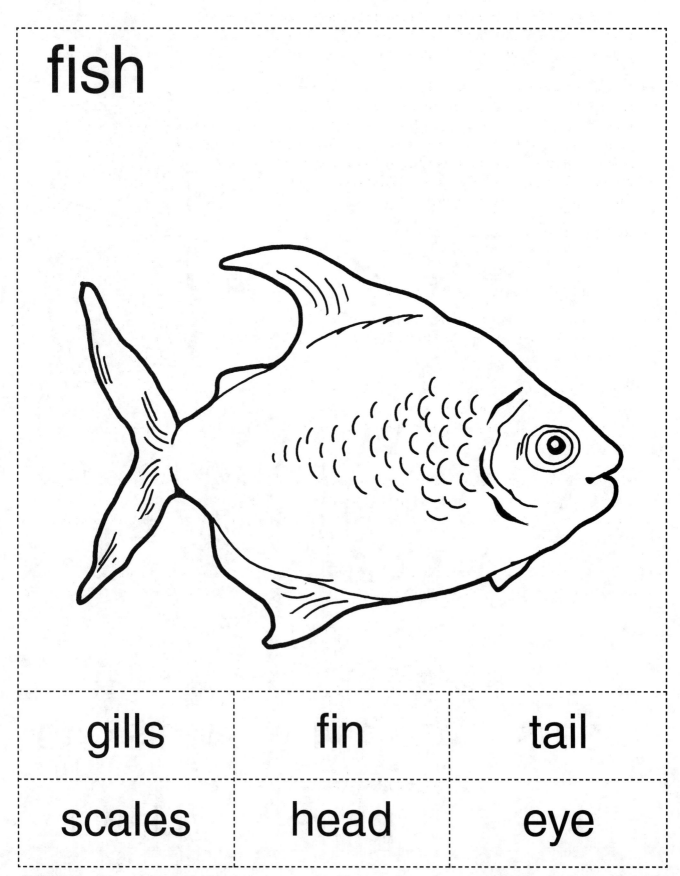

gills	fin	tail
scales	head	eye

Post Office

Lead Ins

- Ask the children about the kind of mail that comes to their homes. Make a list of the different kinds—birthday cards, holiday cards, newspapers, invitations, junk mail, bills, advertisements, packages, etc. Bring a large stack of mail to group time and have children sort it with you.

- Discuss packaging. Show samples of an envelope, an express mail cardboard envelope, a mailing tube, and a box. Discuss the different uses for each item. Show an array of items (a child's drawing or a poster, a gift, a letter, a glass, etc.) and ask which type packaging would work best. Take turns placing items in appropriate containers. Demonstrate how to roll the posters to fit in tubes. Give each child a sheet of paper to practice rolling.

- Ask the following questions.

  Why do we wrap packages?

  What kinds of packaging materials are best?

  What does *fragile* mean? Share examples of different packing materials. Demonstrate how to package something fragile to protect it.

- Discuss different ways mail is delivered—by foot, by truck, by plane. Poll the class to determine how each child gets his or her mail. Does it come through a mail slot in the front door, to a mailbox by the street, to a post office box? Discuss the red flag on some mailboxes. What does it mean?

- Share different stamps. Look at the designs and the prices. You may want to show a real stamp collection at this time. Encourage children to collect cancelled stamps from mail that comes to their homes. Start a display and add to it on a daily basis. Later, the stamps can be used for sorting activities.

Hint: The Post Office center works well anytime of year, but many educators find it particularly useful around Valentine's Day or during the winter holidays when there are so many cards and packages being sent.

Post Office *(cont.)*

Suggested Materials for the Post Office

- air mail envelopes
- bubble wrap
- cardboard tubes (toilet paper, wrapping paper, and paper towel)
- cards and envelopes
- children's books related to getting letters, mail, and/or the post office
- computer and keyboard
- envelopes
- envelopes with cancelled stamps
- express mail envelopes
- index cards (colored)
- junk mail
- blank labels
- letters
- mail bags
- mail boxes
- milk cartons
- money (pages 246–247)
- packaging materials
- scales
- shoe boxes
- stamps and stamp pads
- postage stamps
- stickers
- tape (cellophane, masking, packing)
- wagon or cart
- writing implements

Post Office *(cont.)*

Teacher Preparation

1. Set up a service counter in the Post Office. Arrange postage stamps, ink stamps, stamp pads, a measuring scale, a supply of different kinds of envelopes, and cardboard packing tubes. If available, add an old computer to the service area.

2. Establish a writing area. Stock the writing area with large and small envelopes, stickers, felt pens, cards, postcards, index cards, etc. Display different types of mail on the wall. Include properly addressed envelopes and packages. Encourage the children to write letters and postcards at the writing center. These can be used in the Post Office when it is their turn to play. Consider having them dictate letters to family members that can be sent home at the end of the day.

3. Arrange an area to prepare packages. Include boxes of different sizes, packing material, brown paper, cardboard tubes, ink stamps, stamp pads, different kinds of tape, and a scale. Encourage children to pack, weigh, and wrap their boxes. Add labels (page 93) and addresses.

4. Gather or create uniform items to go with the character nametags, such as baseball caps for the mail carriers and blue vests (see page 251) for the sorters and clerks.

5. Cut squares of paper using pinking shears to create jagged edges. Invite students to use the paper to design their own commemorative stamps. Display each child's stamp in the post office with an explanation of its design.

6. Establish a price list with the children for items and services in the post office. Place a roll of adding machine tape next to the cash register so the checker can tear off receipts for the customer. Make money appropriate for the price list.

7. Create numbered post office boxes in one area of the Post Office. Collect a quart milk carton for each student in the class. Cut off the top and bottom of each cartons and show them to the children. Explain that you are trying to make post office boxes and work with them to create a stable arrangement. For instance, if you have twenty cartons, you might place five on the bottom row and stack three more rows of five on top. Staple or glue the cartons together.
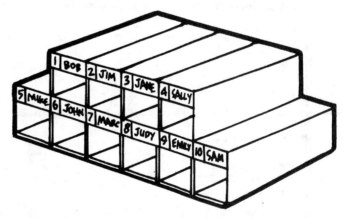
Number each box. Assign each child a box. Beside the boxes, post a list of the numbers and the names of the owners. Assign one box for the class and put announcements and messages in it. Assign a different child to check the box each day. Use the box to announce special events, guests, and birthday announcements, etc.

8. Work with children to label different areas of the classroom with addresses. Place a mailbox at each address. Encourage children to add additional addresses as the Post Office center progresses.

9. Plan a trip to the Post Office or ask the school mail carrier to come in on a special day. Prearrange to have a surprise package or letter delivered that day.

Post Office *(cont.)*

Student Preparation

1. Name the Post Office after your town or city. Create a sign for the Post Office. Decorate the sign with items found in a post office. Create additional signs for the Writing Area and the Packaging Area.

2. Collect junk mail and advertisements. Cut them up into interesting shapes and create a collage to decorate the Post Office.

3. Create a mail truck using a box. Add headlights, wheels, etc., and label the sides and back. Use a pipe cleaner for an antennae. Attach shoulder straps so that it can be worn. Attach a shoe box bottom to the inside of the mail truck to hold the mail as deliveries are made. (Alternative: Add labels to a wagon or cart instead.)

4. Design mail bags for the mail carriers. Add labels to backpacks or large tote bags or collect plain-colored shopping bags with handles and decorate them with pictures of mail carriers.

5. Encourage each child to design a personal mailbox using a shoebox. Have each child add personal pictures and his or her name. Attach a red flag to the side using a brad. Use them around the room, in cubbies, or for a special event, such as holding valentines.

6. Create postcards to be mailed or sold in the post office. Draw pictures on one side of colored index cards. Divide the other side in half with a vertical line. Use the left side for a message and the right side for the address and a stamp.

Vocabulary Building

air mail	mail bag	package
delivery	mailbox	packaging materials
envelope	mail carrier	post office
express mail	overnight	scale
fragile	postal	special delivery
junk mail	post office box	stamps
letter	P. O. Box	

Post Office *(cont.)*

Literacy Development

- Have the children practice their writing skills by writing postcards and letters, addressing envelopes, and labeling boxes and packages. Have younger children dictate letters or thank you notes.

- Take this opportunity to make class thank you cards to special classroom helpers. Walk with the children to a mailbox and mail the cards. Make this a regular ritual in your classroom.

- Preparing packages for mailing is a good opportunity for children to use descriptive words for size (*tiny, small, medium, large, huge, gigantic*) and opposites (*big/little, large/small, heavy/light,* etc.). Make a list of size words for the center and add to it as new words are learned.

- Add addresses and labels (page 93) to packages.

- Create a class address book. Print the addresses beside each child's name and/or picture. Post the list in the writing/craft area. Encourage students to copy the numbers and letters that form an address. You may wish to write only the street addresses at first.
  Safety Note: Check with parents before posting addresses.

Numeracy Development

- Have the mail carriers count incoming and outgoing mail. They can match numbers on addresses when delivering mail.

- Have the mail sorters place numbered index cards in appropriate post office boxes each day. They can divide up stacks of advertisements and junk mail so that each post office box receives a similar amount.

- Have postal clerks sell stamps and packing envelopes. They can weigh and measure packages, determine the number of stamps, affix stamps to envelopes, and assign prices. Before beginning the Post Office, mark the scale equating certain weights with certain stamp amounts 1 lb. (.5 kg) equals one stamp, 2lbs.(1 kg) equals two stamps.

- Work on size concepts (heavy, heavier, heaviest; small, smaller, smallest, etc.). Fill boxes with different materials and compare them. Use objects in the classroom to compare sizes and weights. Another option is to mail packages by box size. If a package fits in one size box it will cost $1; if it fits in the next size box, it will be $2.

- Customers can make use of many math skills when preparing their letters and packages. Finding the right size envelope for a card or letter can be made into a game.

Post Office *(cont.)*

Character Nametags

Package Labels

Special Delivery

Fragile	Overnight

Express Mail

Repair Shop

Lead Ins

- Ask your children if they know what a repair shop is or if any of them have ever been to one. Make a list of things that break and need to be repaired. (Consider cars, machines, vacuums, lamps, jewelry, glasses, computers, etc.)

- Display the pieces of a flashlight that has been taken apart. Ask children what they think it is and how it can be fixed. Count and name the parts—light bulb, casing, lens, batteries, spring, on/off switch. Have the children help you put it back together again. Explain that when things need to be repaired they often have to be taken apart to figure out what is wrong. Tell them that they will have opportunities to take things apart in the Repair Shop.

- Discuss different tools that might be used to repair a broken item. Share a variety of tools and demonstrate how to use them. Compare different types of pliers and screwdrivers.

- Introduce pictures of tools, labels, and nametags for the repair shop.

- Bring in a broken item, preferably one with an electrical cord. Discuss the item and how it is used. Explain that, for safety reasons, the cord and plug will be cut off the item. Take the item apart with the students. Take turns using the tools. Focus on the different components and on where parts are connected. Sort the different parts that have been removed. Explain that, in this case, the item is not going to be put back together but that the parts will be saved and sorted. During the last week of the Repair Shop, have the children use all the parts and pieces of disassembled items to create a robot or collage.

Safety Note: Remind the students that they will have a special opportunity in the Repair Shop dramatic play center to take things apart, but that they should not do this at home without permission. Remind them that they should never cut electrical cords off of anything.

Suggested Materials for the Repair Shop

- broken appliances (blenders, toasters, vacuums)
- cash register or money box
- children's books about machines, repairs, and "how things work"
- flat-edge screwdrivers
- household repair books
- magazines about machinery, tools, appliances
- magnets
- magnifiers
- money (pages 246–247)
- nuts and bolts (different sizes)
- old bicycles
- old computers
- old keyboards
- old lamps
- old phones (rotary phones are the best!)
- old stereos
- pegboard or bulletin board with hooks
- Phillips head screwdrivers
- pliers
- safety glasses and goggles
- screws
- tape
- aluminum foil
- tool belt
- tool box
- tools
- wire cutters

Teacher Note: The older the appliances, the better. Old record players, TVs and rotary phones are filled with screws, knobs, and multi-colored wires that are interesting to disassemble. Newer appliances have more computer chips and fewer nuts and bolts.

Repair Shop (cont.)

Teacher Preparation

1. Create a Workbench Area in the Repair Shop. Arrange tools, safety glasses or goggles, and an item or two to take apart. Check all donated, old, or broken appliances. Make sure that all cords have been cut off and that there are no sharp edges. Post the safety signs (page 99).

2. Display other donated items that will be taken apart or "repaired" at a later date. If possible, hang the tools on hooks attached to pegboards or bulletin boards with labels below them.

3. The repair shop can be a wonderfully exciting dramatic play center. The type of tools offered and the objects to be disassembled will determine the amount of adult supervision required at the workbench. It can also be a venue to teach or reinforce a variety of safety rules.

   —Remind children that adults are in charge of plugging in machines and turning them on and off.

   —Require workers at the workbench in the Repair Shop to wear safety goggles.

4. Create a reception area where customers can bring in items and also pay for repairs. Set up a cash register or money box and work with the children to establish a price sheet.

5. Enlarge, color, and laminate the tool pictures on pages 101–103. Cut them up to form puzzles with interlocking pieces. Determine how many pieces per puzzle and the degree of difficulty.

6. Make additional puzzles using large, laminated pictures of machines and appliances. **Optional:** Mount the pictures on cardboard for ease in handling.

7. Make an inventory list of all the tools and goggles. Post the list near the workbench. Have the participants check the list at the beginning and the end of their turn in the Repair Shop.

8. Label boxes and store them under the workbench. One box might be for nuts, bolts, and screws. Another might be for wires and belts and another box for computer cards or chips. Determine the labels based on the types of items being dismantled. As boxes fill up, sort them again. Separate the nuts from the bolts, the copper wire from the covered wire, etc. Explain that the parts collected will be used to create a robot or perhaps to make a new invention.

9. When a significant number of parts have accumulated, set aside space in the craft area where children can use the parts and incorporate them into collages, new inventions, and other art works.

10. Be very clear with children that it is okay to take apart specific items in the Repair Shop, but that they should "not try this at home!"

11. Try to arrange a visit to a repair shop or to have a visitor skilled in repair work come to visit the class. Ask the guest to bring a sampling of his or her most useful tools.

Special Note: The children may notice that they are taking things apart more than they are repairing them. Explain that, in order to fix things, it is important to learn how they work. By taking things apart, one can see how they are put together. There could be a broken part or a part that is worn out. The more that a repair person knows about how something works, the better chance that he or she can fix it.

Repair Shop *(cont.)*

Student Preparation

1. Create a sign for the Repair Shop. Decorate it with stickers or pictures of tools. Make additional signs for the workbench and tool areas.

2. Match the tool pictures with actual tools. If additional tools are available for the shop, try to find matching pictures in magazines.

3. Cut out pictures of machines, cars, appliances, and other items that can break and be repaired. Make a collage.

4. Sort a collection of nuts and bolts. Find the matching bolt for each nut and screw it on. Unscrew all the nuts and bolts and return them to the box for the next person.

5. Make a set of number tags or claim checks for each item that comes into the shop.

6. Draw pictures of tools and machines. Make stories or create puzzles to go along with them.

7. Make an Open/Closed sign (page 245) for the shop. Decorate it with pictures from tool catalogs.

Vocabulary Building

automatic	magnets	replace
bolt	magnifiers	ruler
broken	measuring tape	safety glasses
claim check	nut	scale
damaged	on	tape
electrical	off	tool belt
fixed	Phillips head screwdrivers	tools
flat-edge screwdrivers	pliers	wire cutters
goggles	receipt	workbench
inventory	repair	worn out

Repair Shop *(cont.)*

Literacy Component

- Help children make a list of all the tools in the shop. Indicate how many of each tool is available.

- Discuss what each tool is used for in the shop. Clap out the syllables for the name of each tool. Return each tool to its proper place at the end of each shift in the repair shop.

- Have children trace the tools on white paper. Color in the outlines. Make a class book or individual books of tool pictures. Encourage children to add pages about their favorite tools and find or draw pictures of them.

- Make a list of tools that help people do things more safely or more easily (sewing machine, lawn mower, scissors, etc.). Write a class essay about how tools help people.

- Encourage children to describe how an item in the repair shop is supposed to work. Describe what it is and its purpose. Discuss what might be inside to make the machine work. Once the casing for the machine has been removed, describe what has been uncovered. Look at the different parts. Are the pieces shiny, smooth, interlocking, small, large, etc.? If desired, write down what the children share. Create books or posters for the shop detailing the discoveries.

- Create a robot using pieces removed from the different items in the repair shop. Begin by covering two or three large boxes with aluminum foil. Stack the boxes and glue them together. Lay the connected boxes down on a flat surface. Have the children use glue or tape to add screws, plastic pieces, computer cards, old CDs, switches, etc. Create antennae using wire or old knobs. When the robot is complete, have the children write or dictate stories about it. Have them illustrate the stories and display them in the classroom.

- Play games to reinforce the concepts of ON and OFF. Play a version of Freeze Tag indoors. When the light is turned off, children can move around very slowly, when the light goes on they need to FREEZE. Outside, draw lines, boxes, or other markings on the pavement. When the leader yells ON, everyone must find a line or a box to stand on. When the leader yells OFF, children are free to walk, hop, or run around.

Numeracy Component

- Attach number tags to each item in the store. Use the tags on page 100. Periodically check on the progress of a specific item. "Can you tell me when #5 will be ready?" "Do you think #8 can be fixed or is it beyond repair?"

- Sort and count all the screws, bolts, wires, and other items removed from appliances at the repair shop.

- Take daily inventory in the shop. How many machines need to be repaired/taken apart?

- Compare the number of parts in different items. Weigh and measure them. Use standard and nonstandard measurement tools.

- Start a contest to find the largest screw or bolt, the longest piece of wire, the heaviest piece of metal, etc. Add new winners as they are discovered.

Repair Shop (cont.)

Character Nametags

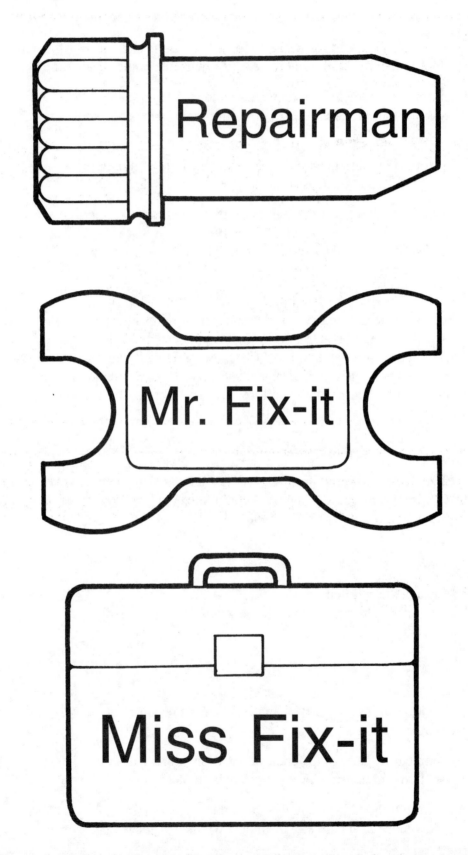

Repair Shop *(cont.)*

Safety Signs

Always wear safety goggles!

Use tools with care.

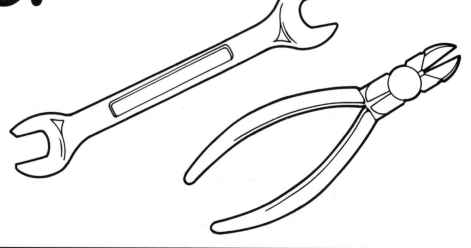

Repair Shop *(cont.)*

Repair Tags and Receipts

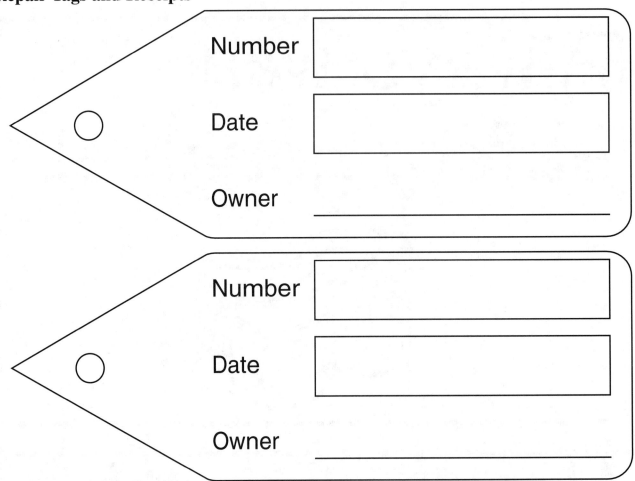

| Number |
| Date |
| Owner |

| Number |
| Date |
| Owner |

Receipt

Number

Problem

Owner

Receipt

Number

Problem

Owner

Repair Shop *(cont.)*

Tools

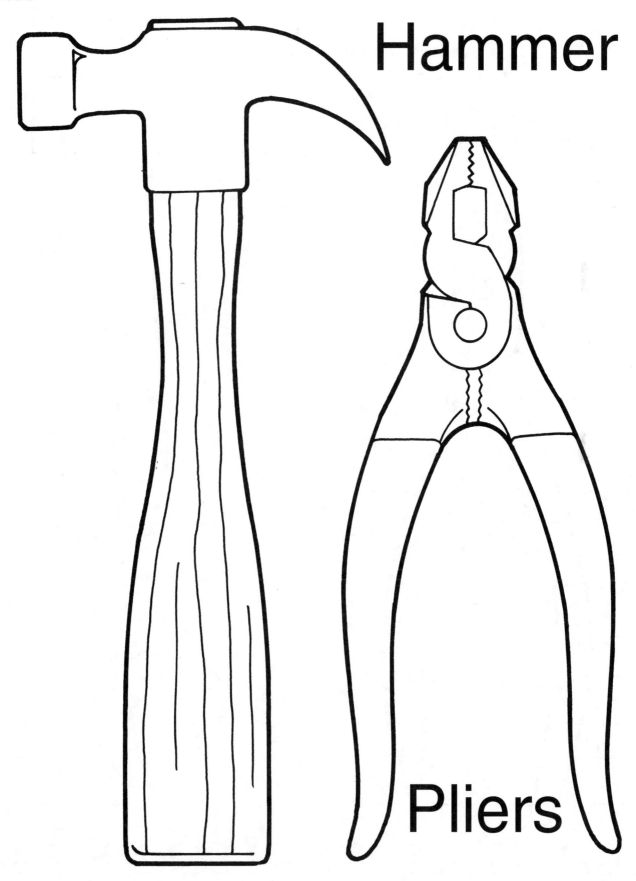

Hammer

Pliers

Tools (*cont.*)

Wire Cutters

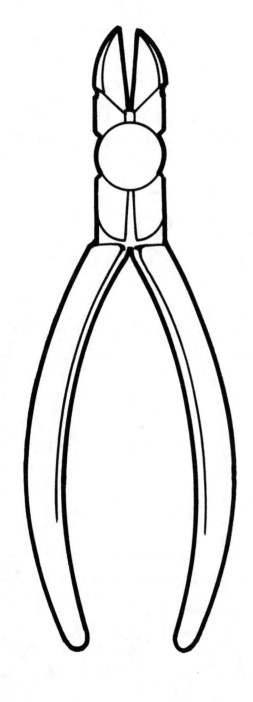

Wrench

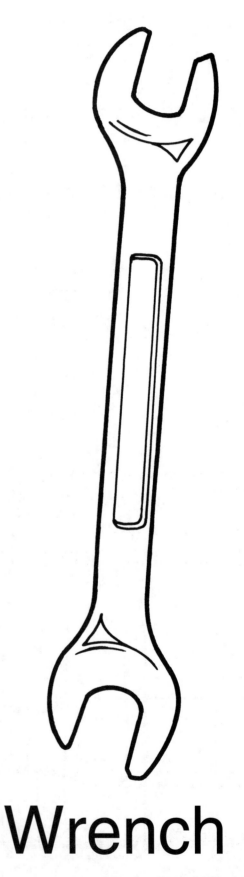

Repair Shop *(cont.)*

Tools

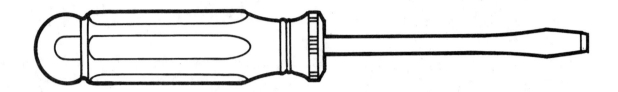

flat edge screwdriver—small

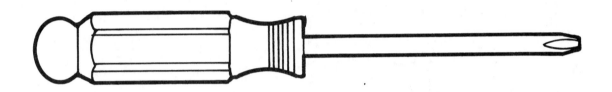

Phillips Head screwdriver—small

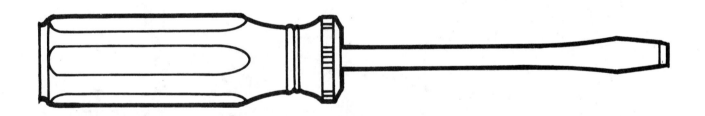

flat edge screwdriver—large

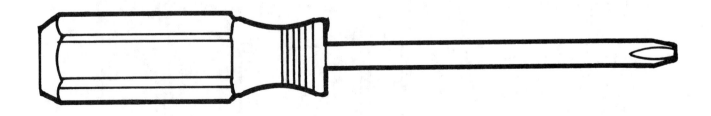

Phillips Head screwdriver—large

Restaurant

Lead Ins

- Be sure to make the distinction between a restaurant with a drive-thru window and a more formal one when presenting this dramatic play center. Explain that you are talking about restaurants where there is a person who comes to your table and takes your order, later brings you your food, and finally gives you a check for the meal.

- You may wish to have children tell you about their favorite restaurants. Discuss what is on the table, how they determine what they will eat, what the décor is like, who cooks, who cleans up, and how the food arrives at the table.

- Discuss the occasions when families go to restaurants—to celebrate a special occasion, when there isn't time to cook dinner, after a sporting event, for a special treat, etc.

- Ask if there are rules for eating at restaurants that are different from eating at home. Discuss manners. Create a list of proper table manners. Post the list.

Suggested Materials for the Restaurant

- adding machine tape
- aprons
- cash register or money box
- chef hats
- cloth napkins
- computer and keyboard
- dress-up clothes for customers
- flowers for the tables
- folders or large construction paper
- menus (pages 111–113)
- microphone (page 250)
- money (pages 246–247)
- notepads (for orders)
- plastic dishes
- plastic food
- plastic silverware
- pots and pans
- restaurant menus
- stove
- tablecloths
- telephone

Restaurant *(cont.)*

Teacher Preparation

1. Set up a shelf or counter for the cooking/food prep area, a table or two for patrons, and an area for the cashier. Set up the cash register and/or computer monitor and keyboard. Place a roll of adding machine tape beside the cash register so the cashier can tear off receipts for the customers. Set up a microphone to page guests when their tables are ready.

2. Consider making place mats for the restaurant by tracing the dishes, cups, napkins, and silverware on construction paper. Laminate the place mats and demonstrate for the children where each piece goes. Incorporate concepts of left and right to this shape matching process. **Example:** The fork goes on the left side of the plate (large circle). The knife and the spoon go on the right side of the plate.

3. Make labels for the restaurant and nametags for the participants (pages 108–109). Determine ahead of time how many chefs, customers, food servers (waiters and waitresses), etc., your restaurant can accommodate and make the appropriate number of nametags. Discuss the different employee roles.

   Managers/Maitre d's are responsible for seating customers, running the restaurant, and handling any problems that may arise.

   Food servers (waiters and waitresses) take customers' orders, bring the food, and tally the checks.

   Busboys and Bussers take care of the tables. They set them and clear them after customers leave.

   Chefs prepare the food when the waiter or waitress turns in his or her order.

   Cashiers take the checks and the money and make change for the customers.

4. Establish a seating capacity for the restaurant. Post the number at the entrance to the restaurant or place numbers at each table—table for 1, 2, 4, etc. Number cards can be found in the Appendix on pages 242–244.

5. Determine a maximum number of participants in the kitchen prep area and place a number card under the Kitchen sign to remind children. Number cards can be found in the Appendix on pages 242–244.

6. Discuss the importance of hand washing before preparing or eating food. Design a reminder sign or use the one on page 114.

7. Plan costume options for the restaurant workers. Chefs can wear labeled painters caps or obtain chefs hats from a local restaurant or restaurant supply house. Food servers (waiters and waitresses) can wear aprons and carry menu pads. Managers might wear suit jackets or vests, etc.

8. Plan menus for the restaurant with the children. Determine ahead of time if the food served will come from the pretend food in the housekeeping area, laminated pictures of food items, or if the food will be imaginary. Choose five or six favorite items to be printed on a menu or use the menus provided on pages 111–113.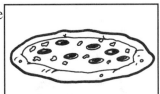

9. Establish prices for the menu items. Create appropriate money using the patterns on pages 246–247. Make credit cards and checkbooks too! (Use pages 248–249.)

10. Plan a trip to a restaurant as a culminating event for the center.

Restaurant (cont.)

Student Preparation

1. Choose a name for the restaurant and make a large sign for the area. Write out the name in large bubble-type letters and color them in or decorate them with glitter, collage materials, etc.

2. Decorate menu covers. Use folders, folded construction paper, or the patterns on page 111. Place copies of the menus inside.

3. Review table manners using the list created during discussion time. After the list is written and decorated, post it in the classroom. Take turns demonstrating proper and improper behavior during a meal.

4. Practice ordering from the menus during group time. There are two types of menu options provided. One is pictorial and one includes prices. Food servers (waiters and waitresses) using either menu can circle the correct choices.

5. Review the labels and character nametags.

6. Practice folding napkins and setting the tables.

7. Cover cans or decorate large cups and label them to store plastic knives, forks, and spoons.

8. Decorate an Open/Closed sign (page 245) for the restaurant.

Vocabulary Building

appetizer	cook	maitre d'
breakfast	customer	menu
brunch	credit card	patrons
busboy	dessert	restaurant
bussers	diner	snack
cashier	dinner	special of the day
cash register	gratuity	tip
check	kitchen	waiter
chef	lunch	waitress

Note: Add menu items to the center vocabulary list.

Restaurant *(cont.)*

Literacy Development

- Use the menu template on page 111 to create a menu for the restaurant. Print the menu items and add prices (see Numeracy Development). Make additional copies of the menus. Encourage the waiter or waitress to use the menus when taking orders. Have them turn in the "circled" or "checked" menus to the chef. The chef, in turn, can "read" the menus while preparing the food.

- Decorate the restaurant with pictures of food the children have cut out of magazines. Help them label the pictures. Keep magazines and paper for labeling handy so children can add to the food pictures throughout the life of the center.

- Vote on a new special entrée each day and post it at the entrance to the restaurant near the menus.

- Practice "left" and "right" when putting silverware on the table.

- Work on sequencing skills. Which meal comes first in a day—breakfast, lunch, or dinner? When do you have snacks? Do you have dessert before or after a meal?

- Discuss the word *brunch*. What does it mean and what two words were combined to make the word brunch (breakfast and lunch)? What is the difference between dinner and supper?

- Discuss the meaning of the words *tip* and *gratuity*.

- Have each child create a mini book of favorite foods. Supply blank books and have them add illustrations, magazine pictures, etc. Rank the foods with star stickers. One star for a good food, two stars for a special treat, and three stars for the absolute favorite food in the book.

Numeracy Development

- Work with children to determine pricing for the restaurant. Post an enlarged copy of the menu at the entrance to the restaurant. For children who are just beginning to learn the number symbols, keep it simple: $1, $2, etc. For more advanced children, use more accurate prices: $1.00, $2.50.

- Explain the placement of the period and the zeros when writing prices. Offer children ample time to practice writing prices. You may wish to have children trace the prices on the worksheet on page 115.

- Keep track of the silverware. At the end of each shift in the restaurant, take turns counting the knives, forks, spoons etc., to make sure all have been returned to the storage containers.

- Encourage the children to add up the totals on the meal checks and pay accordingly. Don't forget about making change and about tipping.

Restaurant *(cont.)*

Character Nametags

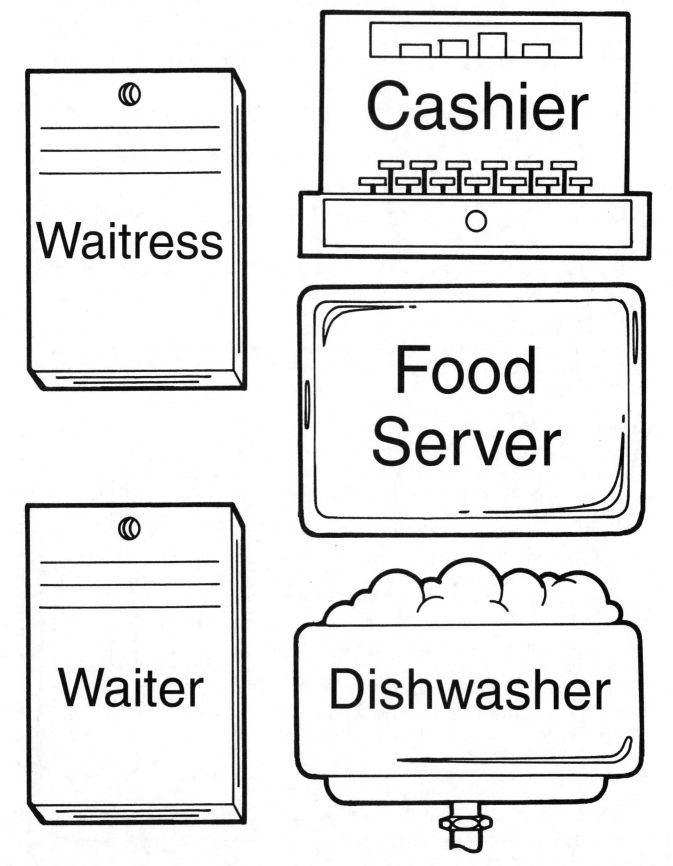

Restaurant *(cont.)*

Characters Nametags *(cont.)*

Chef

Busser

Maitre d'

Manager

Restaurant *(cont.)*

Directions to teacher: Once the menu items have been chosen, add the appropriate pictures to the menu templates below. Make copies for the children and explain usage.

Sample Order Pad 1

Circle the items that the customers order.

Sample Order Pad 2

Place a check near the item each customers order.

Menu

Menu

Restaurant *(cont.)*

Menu Cover

Fill in the name of the restaurant and cut out the frame. Use colored paper to make copies of the cover. On separate pieces of paper, create menus. Use the pictures on pages 112–113 or use cutouts from magazines or newspapers. Add prices if appropriate. Staple the cover to the menu.

Option: Attach the cover and menu pages to file folders and laminate the menus for durability.

Menu

_____

Restaurant

Restaurant *(cont.)*

Menu Options

bacon

pizza

fried eggs

sausage

hamburger

scrambled eggs

hot dog

soup

Restaurant *(cont.)*

chicken

juice

coffee

milk

French fries

steak

grilled cheese

taco

Food Safety Signs

Wash your hands before eating.

Wash your hands before cooking.

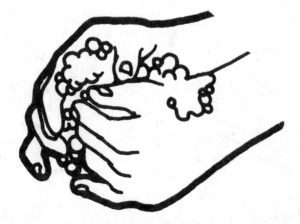

Restaurant *(cont.)*

Price Worksheet

Directions: Trace the words and the prices on the worksheet. Circle your favorite food item.

hamburger	$3.00
hot dog	$1.25
pizza	$1.75
grilled cheese	$3.00
juice	40¢
milk	50¢

Shoe Store

Lead Ins

- Shoe shopping is always fun and children love the dress-up aspect of it. To start, have all the children come to group time, take off their shoes, and place them in front of them as they sit down. Discuss how many shoes each person wears. Ask what another way of saying "two shoes" might be. Discuss the meaning of the word *pair*.

- Place a pile of the children's shoes or the shoes donated for the dramatic play center in the middle of the group. (If the group is large, consider making two piles for two separate groups.) Invite the children to sort through the piles and find pairs of shoes. After the shoes have all been matched, discuss where shoes are sold.

- Discuss shoe sizes. Ask if any of the children know their shoe sizes. Group the children by shoe size and graph the classes' shoe sizes. Mention that adult shoe sizes have the same numbers as children's sizes, but that they are larger than children's shoes. Compare an adult size to a child's size with the same number.

- Discuss how feet are measured in a shoe store. Explain that shoes come in special sizes and widths. Introduce the foot measurement tool that will be used in the store (pages 125).

- Discuss "left" and "right." Refer to left and right hands, left and right feet, etc., whenever possible. Place small circular stickers on children's left or right feet to help them remember which is which. Do the "Hokey Pokey" to practice right and left.

- Read a version of *The Elves and the Shoemaker* and discuss how shoes used to be made by hand. Discuss how shoes are made in modern times.

Suggested Materials for the Shoe Store

- cash register or money box
- dress-up clothes for customers
- foot measurement patterns (page 125)
- lacing activity cards
- magazines and store catalogs with shoe pictures
- measurement worksheet (page 124)
- money (pages 246–247)
- purses
- sales receipt notepads
- shoe boxes
- shoe laces—all colors and kinds
- shoe horns
- shoes—all kinds and sizes (babies, children's, men's, and women's)
- shoe store and sporting goods store advertisements
- socks
- telephone
- vests

Shoe Store *(cont.)*

Teacher Preparation

1. Set up shelves to display the different shoes. Plan with the children whether to arrange the shoes by size or by use. Place each pair in a shoebox, if available. Have children find the appropriate lid for each box of shoes.

2. Make labels for the shoe store and nametags for the participants (pages 121–122). Determine ahead of time how many sales clerks, customers, and stock personnel your store can accommodate and make nametags to suit.

3. Establish prices for the shoes. Enlist the children's help putting a price tag on each box of shoes. Have a sale when children become accustomed to the prices. Change the prices from time to time.

4. Determine a maximum number of participants and place a capacity card under the store sign to remind the children. Number cards can be found in the Appendix on page 242–244.

5. Gather or create uniform items to go with the character nametags. Vests, sport coats, or other "business attire" from the dress up collections would be appropriate.

6. Make sets of matching shoe picture cards to create concentration games or color and laminate the cards on page 122–123. Enlarge the cards to suit class needs.

7. Discuss the importance of wearing socks when trying on shoes. Make it a rule that socks must be worn to try on shoes in the store.

8. Make a path of footprints in the classroom (or outside) for children to walk on. Place the footprints in a regularly used path. It could lead to the snack table, to the bathroom, or to the coat hooks. Label each left foot with an **L** and each right foot with an **R**. Encourage them to say "Left" when they step on a left foot and "Right" when they step on a right foot all the way along the path.

9. Set up lacing activity cards for children. Punch holes around the edges of paper plates and supply shoelaces for the children to weave in an out of the holes. Copy the template below onto colored poster board. Punch where marked and laminate it to allow children to practice lacing shoes.

Shoe Lacing Template

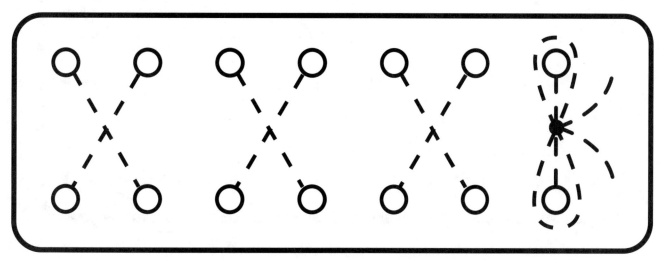

Shoe Store *(cont.)*

Student Preparation

1. Decide on a name for the shoe store. The students might want to name it after the street that the school is located on or to give it the same name as the school. Use a large sheet of paper shaped like a shoe or a shoehorn to make the sign for the shoe store. Color in letter outlines stating the name of the store or outline the letters by gluing brightly colored shoelaces on the lines.

2. Sort the donated shoes into groups. Try sorting by the age of the person who might wear them (baby, child, teenager, adult) or by use (sports, dress, everyday, slippers, etc.). The shoes could also be sorted into groups for men, women, and children.

3. Create individual books with pictures of favorite shoes. Use magazines, catalogs, and store advertisements to find pictures to add to the books.

4. Cut out copies of the sales receipts page (page 126) to make personal sales books. Staple 5 to 10 pages together and make a cover for the book. Use the books in the shoe store when sales are made.

5. Decorate an Open/Closed sign for the shoe store or use the one on page 245. Punch holes around the outside edges of the signs and weave colored shoelaces through the holes for decoration.

Vocabulary Building

boots	left	sizes
cleats	length	slip-ons
dress shoes	loafers	slippers
flats	measure	sneakers
flip flops	pair	socks
high heels	party shoes	sport shoes
high tops	right	tennis shoes
laces	shoelaces	tie
lay-away	shoes	width
leather	shoe horn	zipper

Shoe Store *(cont.)*

Literacy Component

- Once the concept of *a pair* has been established, make a list of other things that come in pairs. Discuss body parts that come in pairs—eyes, ears, arms, legs, nostrils, etc. Name items of clothing that come in pairs—shoes, socks, mittens, and gloves. Discuss why we say *a pair of pants*. Name other items that come in pairs—salt and pepper shakers, bookends, tires on a bicycle, twins, etc. Keep lists and add to them during the use of the center. Create a "Pairs" display area.

- After the first week of the Shoe Shop dramatic play center, make sorting shoes by pairs a little more difficult. Place three or four pairs of shoes in a large bag. Have the children take turns matching pairs of shoes by touch. Encourage them to describe what they feel as they are searching for matches.

- Sort shoes by style or color. Draw a picture using only the colors on the inside and outside of a chosen shoe.

- Write class stories about shoes in the shop. Pick an unusual shoe or slipper and decide where it came from, who wore it, what they did while wearing it, etc. Be creative. Tell a different story about a different shoe and begin with the words, "Once upon a time in the land of shoes, there was a..."

- Perform a puppet show using shoes as puppets. Consider making or drawing faces on the soles of the shoes. Have the puppeteers place their hands inside the shoes to maneuver them.

- Enlarge a set of the shoe cards on pages 122–123. Hold up different cards and ask the children to identify the kind of shoe they see. Discuss the different words used to describe a kind of shoe. Tennis shoes can also be called "running shoes" or "sneakers." Basketball shoes are often called "high-tops" and girls' party shoes are sometimes known as "Mary Janes." Discuss additional terms used in your area.

- Note the two most common shoe colors in the class and create a Venn diagram. Have each student participating write his or her name or place an appropriate mark or sticky note in the area of the diagram representing his or her shoe color.

- Place a large letter **L** and a large letter **R** on the floor. Sort all the shoes into two piles, one for left shoes and one for right shoes. Put one color dot sticker on all the *left* shoes and another color sticker on all the *right* shoes.

- Have everyone take off his or her left shoe and hop on his or her right foot and vice versa.

- Play guessing games. "I am thinking of a kind of shoe that you wear to a party, to play baseball, to dance, etc." Once the children get the idea, let them play among themselves. For a variation, use the shoe cards on page 122–123 as prompts.

Shoe Store *(cont.)*

Numeracy Component

- Assist each child in tracing his or her own foot (or shoe). Cut out the foot and use it to measure items in the classroom. If appropriate, have the children complete the measurement worksheet on page 124.

- Line up pairs of shoes from the shop or from the children. Practice skip counting (2, 4, 6, 8) when counting pairs of shoes. Increase the number of pairs to be counted as children improve.

- Arrange the shoes by size. Count how many pairs of shoes are longer or shorter than a certain measurement tool—an eraser, a block, a comb, a ruler, etc.

- Line up all the shoes from the smallest one to the largest one. Assign shoe sizes with numbered stickers.

- Compare the longest shoe to the shortest shoe. Rearrange the shoes from tallest (boot) to shortest (sandal). Compare a child's shoe with an adult shoe in the same size.

- Take turns being "Size Detectives." Find something in the room that is longer than, shorter than, or the same size as a specific shoe. Do this a few times, using different shoes.

- Make a graph of the different ways that shoes close (tie, Velcro, slip-on, zipper). Do this once a week and compare the findings. Use the pictures below to enhance the graph.

| tie | slip-on |
| velcro | zipper |

Shoe Store *(cont.)*

Character Nametags

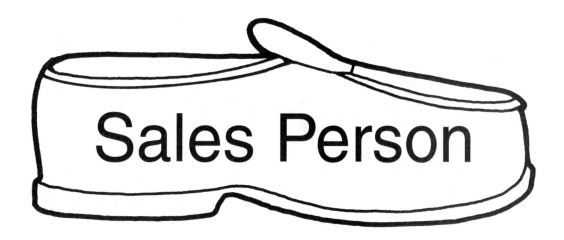

Sales Person

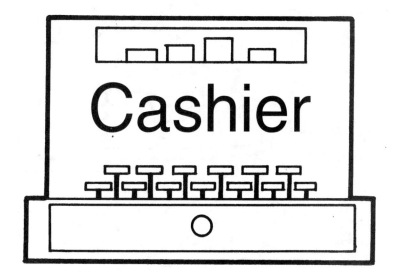

Cashier

Stock Clerk

Shoe Store (cont.)

Store Labels

Shoe Store *(cont.)*

Shoe Cards

Directions: Enlarge the cards and use them in the store or laminate two sets of cards and use them for matching games.

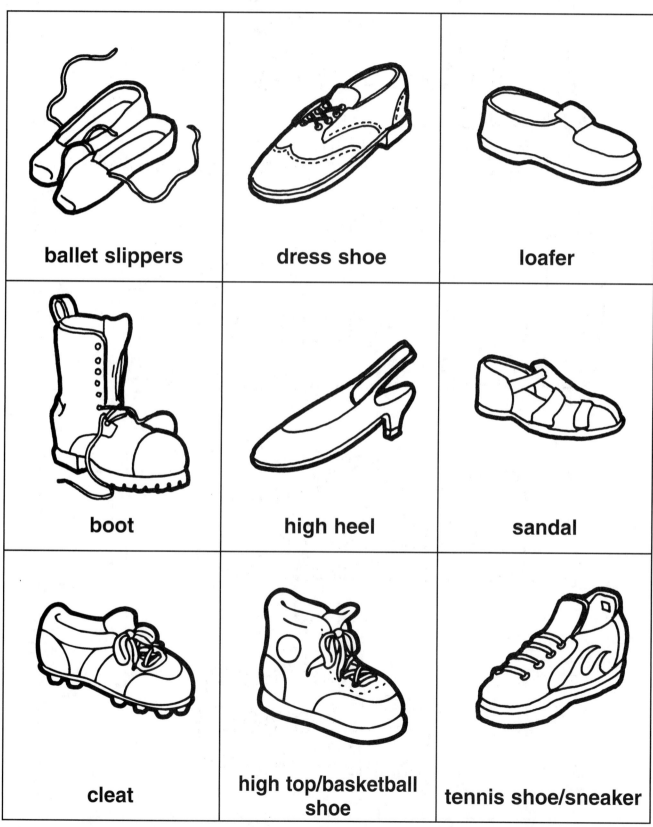

ballet slippers	dress shoe	loafer
boot	high heel	sandal
cleat	high top/basketball shoe	tennis shoe/sneaker

Shoe Store (cont.)

Measurement Worksheet

The _____ is _____ shoes long.

My _____ is _____ shoes long.

The _____ is _____ shoes long.

The _____ is _____ shoes tall.

I am _____ shoes tall.

My teacher is _____ shoes tall.

Shoe Store *(cont.)*

Foot Measurements

Enlarge the patterns below to create two different styles of foot measurements. Choose either the foot or the oval. Make gradual enlargements of the chosen shape on different colors of construction paper to create larger and larger shapes. When you have five or six, cut them out. Arrange them so the largest one is on the bottom of the pile and the smallest is on the top of the pile. Glue them together so the heels are aligned at one end.

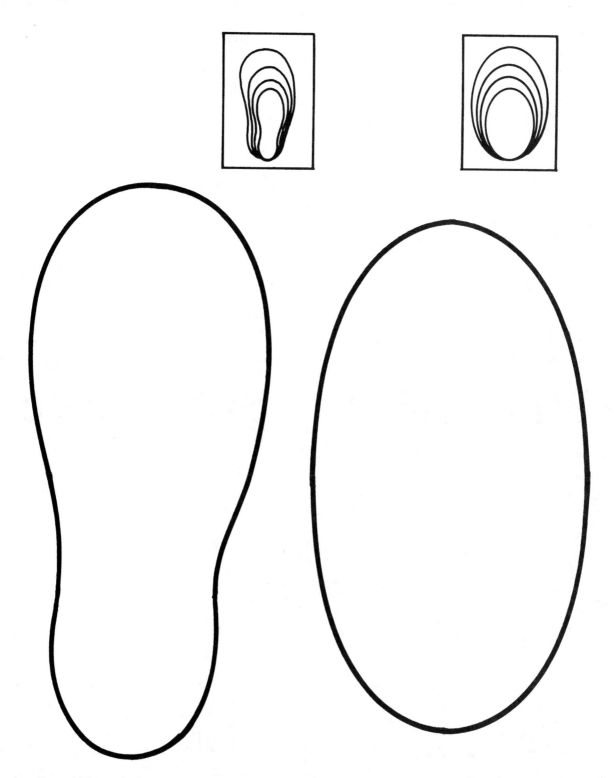

Shoe Store *(cont.)*

Sales Receipts

Shoe Sales	Shoe Sales
Total _____	Total _____
Shoe Sales	Shoe Sales
Total _____	Total _____

Space Travel

Lead Ins

- Discuss different places where children have traveled. Ask how they got to their destinations. Make a chart of all the modes of transportation children have taken.
- Share a picture of a rocket blasting off and ask if anyone has ever traveled to space. Explain that, as a class, they will be taking imaginary journeys to space. Ask what they expect to see. Keep the suggestions in mind when planning future discussions.
- Share a book about the planets. Make a chart of the planets. Put a picture (pages 138–139) and the name of each planet at the beginning of each row. Next to the name of each planet, ask children to contribute facts about it. Does it have rings? Is it a gas planet or a solid planet? Is it cold or hot? (See the sample chart on pages 138–139.) Continue to add information to the chart each day as more is gathered.
- Keep a running list of other things in the solar system that interest the children, such as asteroids, the Milky Way, meteors, black holes, etc.
- Start a Moon Watch. Each day remind the children to look at the moon before they go to sleep at night. The next day, ask what shape (or kind of) moon they saw. Add the correct moon shape to the calendar—no moon, new moon, crescent moon, half moon, or full moon.

Suggested Materials for Space Travel

- children's books about space and space travel
- pipe cleaners in metallic colors
- constellation posters
- duct tape
- freeze dried ice cream and other dehydrated foods
- glitter and glitter pens
- glow-in-the-dark stars
- head sets and old tape recorders
- helmets
- large, empty plastic cola bottles
- computer keyboards
- metallic paper
- metallic crayons
- microphone (page 250)
- mylar blankets (silver emergency blankets)
- old cell phones
- old computers and equipment
- pictures of planets, stars, moons, rockets, etc.
- planet posters
- rain boots
- rubber stamps—circles, stars
- small boxes (jewelry, gelatin, single-serving cereal)
- stamp pads
- Styrofoam balls in different sizes
- telescope
- aluminum foil

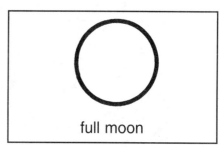

full moon

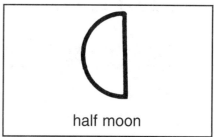

half moon

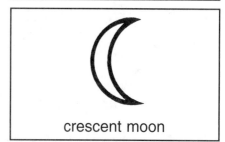

crescent moon

new moon

Space Travel (cont.)

Teacher Preparation

Setting up for space travel can be a bit more involved than other dramatic play centers, but is well worth the effort. The goal is to turn the dramatic play center into the interior of a spaceship. From the ship, the crew can blast off on a new adventure every day. If possible, write a letter at the beginning of the year to NASA requesting the free materials offered for schools. Check the NASA Web site as well (www.NASA.gov).

1. Create low shelves along the walls of the center. These shelves will hold the control panels. To simulate shelves, line the walls with a row of boxes or make shelves with cinder blocks and plywood. Arrange old stereo tuners, PA systems, tape decks, or other machines that have knobs and switches, on the shelves. Place computer keyboards on or near the equipment. Have the children design additional control panels. (See Student Preparation, step 2). If headsets are available use them as well.

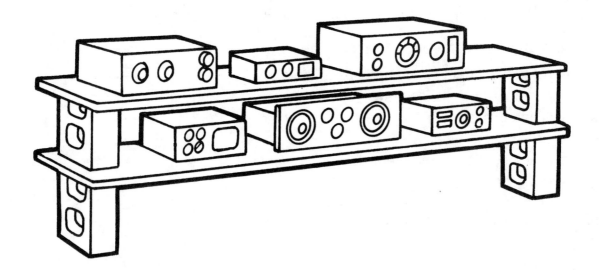

2. Line the walls of the area above the equipment with aluminum foil, mylar blankets, or other silver/gray material.

3. Cut out 12" (30 cm) circle-shaped portholes out of bulletin-board paper (or use large white paper plates). Place one at each crew member's seat around the ship (on top of the aluminum foil). Once the study of space has begun, encourage crew members to draw pictures in the windows showing what they see in space. Change the portholes occasionally as more travel occurs and more information is gathered. Use all of the drawings to make a large book at the end of the center and have the children dictate descriptions.

4. Supply labeled clipboards and writing implements at each station on the rocket ship. (Duplicate the character nametags for the clipboards.) Add constellation and planet maps in the navigation area.

5. Make labels for the different areas on the ship and nametags for the participants. Determine ahead of time the number of astronauts, navigators, and flight crew members your spaceship can accommodate and make copies to suit. Include a Galley Chief to be in charge of snack dispersal if the entire class can fit on board.

Space Travel (cont.)

Teacher Preparation (cont.)

6. Determine a maximum number of participants on board and place a number card at the entrance to remind children. Number cards can be found in the appendix on pages 242–244.

7. Work with the children to make a large rocket using a refrigerator or wardrobe box. Use the box as an additional play center or set it up as the entrance to the center. Cut two identical doors in the lower part of the box to allow the children to walk through the rocket into the center.

8. Gather or create uniform items to go with the character nametags. Make air tanks (page 143). Cover helmets and rain boots with aluminum foil to simulate spacesuit gear.

9. Make a set of planets and a sun using different sized balls. Styrofoam works well and can be painted different colors. Create a display of the planets and suspend them from the ceiling. Place the sun in the center and arrange the planets in orbits around them. Remind the children that the sun is a star, not a planet.

   Hunt: You might wish to start with the sun and add a new planet each day as you discuss outer space during group time. Another option is to discover a new planet each day on a teacher-directed flight in the center.

10. Supply large sheets of black paper, glitter, and metallic paper in the writing/craft area. Offer children opportunities to draw pictures of the solar system using the materials. Later, have them dictate descriptions and/or stories of their creations. Display their work.

11. Invite an astronomer, an astronaut, or someone affiliated with the space program to visit the classroom.

12. Create potato star "stampers" using a star-shaped cookie cutter and potatoes. Simply slice large potatoes in half, press in the cutter and cut around it to create raised, star shapes in the whites of the potatoes.

Space Travel *(cont.)*

Student Preparation

1. Look at different books about space exploration. Decide on a name for the Space Travel dramatic play center and make a sign for the entrance. Consider using white or silver paint on black paper when designing the sign. Decorate it with pictures of planets, stars, satellites, rockets, etc.

2. Design additional control panels for the interior of the center/spaceship. Cover plastic bottle caps with foil and glue them on to covered boxes or large cardboard panels. Color and cut out the gauges found on pages 136–137. Add them to the control panels.

3. Design space helmets and/or spacesuits for costumes. Cover existing bike helmets with aluminum foil and add labels, stickers, or decals. (See page 144 for additional ideas for helmets.)

4. Make a rocket ship from a refrigerator box or a wardrobe box. Get an adult to help shape the top into a point. (See illustration.) Work together to paint the rocket. Lay the box on its side. Paint three sides white or silver on the first day and let it dry. On the second day, roll the box over and paint the remaining side. Add labels. Create a cone shape for the top and cover it with aluminum foil.

5. Create a mural of the constellations. Use black bulletin-board paper, white or metallic paint, and star stamps or potato "stampers." Sprinkle the wet paint with glitter and let the mural dry. Display the mural in the classroom on a wall or the ceiling.

6. Find out more about different planets or other celestial bodies. Plan a visit to one of the places studied. What might be seen there, what weather conditions could be expected, etc.

7. Write or dictate a class letter to NASA asking for items for the classroom dramatic play center. (Do this well in advance of the center's set up to insure timely delivery.)

8. Cover small boxes with aluminum foil and space stickers to make personal "communicators." Use pipe cleaners for antennae.

Vocabulary Building

air	meteor
asteroid	Milky Way
astronaut	moon
atmosphere	Neptune
booster	navigator
countdown	orbit
crater	oxygen
crescent	planets
Earth	Pluto
eclipse	rocket
flight crew	satellite
fuel	Saturn
galaxy	shuttle
galley	space station
gravity	stars
Jupiter	sun
landing	universe
lunar	Uranus
Mars	Venus
Mercury	voyage

Moon Phases

full moon	crescent moon
half moon	new moon

Space Travel *(cont.)*

Literacy Component

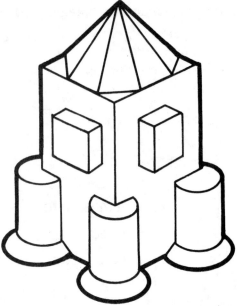

- Review the labels and the character nametags. Choose a few vocabulary words each week and learn more about them. For instance, have each child make a few glittery stars, name them, and create a galaxy for the wall. Name it the Milky Way. Learn the difference between an asteroid and a comet. (Both are celestial bodies, but a comet has a tail.)

- Begin a large chart about the different planets. Incorporate the information on pages 138–139. Add to the chart as new information is learned.

- Make a list of things that would be helpful to have on a space station. Work in small groups and design space stations using blocks and other materials. Take turns sharing information about the designs.

- Learn the names of the planets in order from Mercury, the planet closest to the sun, to Pluto, the farthest planet for which we have information (Mercury, Venus, Earth, Mars, Jupiter, Saturn, Uranus, Neptune, Pluto). Use a pneumonic device to remember the order, such as "**M**y **v**ery **e**xcited **m**other **j**ust **s**erved **u**s **n**ine **p**izzas."

- Have each child choose the planet he or she would most like to live on and tell why. Graph the chosen planets. Which planet is the most popular? Regraph the topic at the end of the dramatic play center's run. Did the results change or remain the same?

- Discuss the difference between the sun, a moon, and a star. Explain that the sun is actually a star. A moon is a satellite of a planet. A planet is a large ball of gas or rock that follows a path (orbit) around the sun.

- Draw or make space exploration vehicles. Dictate or write stories about the vehicles and the voyages they take in the solar system. Add additional stories and create a class book.

Space Travel (cont.)

Numeracy Component

- The countdown is a very important factor in blasting off on a space journey. Count down from 10. Have one of the crew members arrange the number cards so that the zero is on the bottom of the pile and the 10 card is on top. As each number is called out, beginning with 10, that number card is removed. "Ready to countdown—10, 9, 8, 7, 6, 5, 4, 3, 2, 1, 0, BLAST OFF!" If appropriate, add more numbers to the countdown.

- Create a counting game. Make 10 stars, 9 planets, 8 crescent moons, 7 comets, 6 rockets, 5 astronauts, 4 asteroids, 3 shuttles, 2 lunar modules, and 1 sun. Duplicate the patterns on pages 140–142.

- Cut out nine different-sized circles. Label them with the planets names in order from smallest to largest—Pluto, Mercury, Mars, Venus, Earth, Neptune, Uranus, Saturn, and Jupiter.

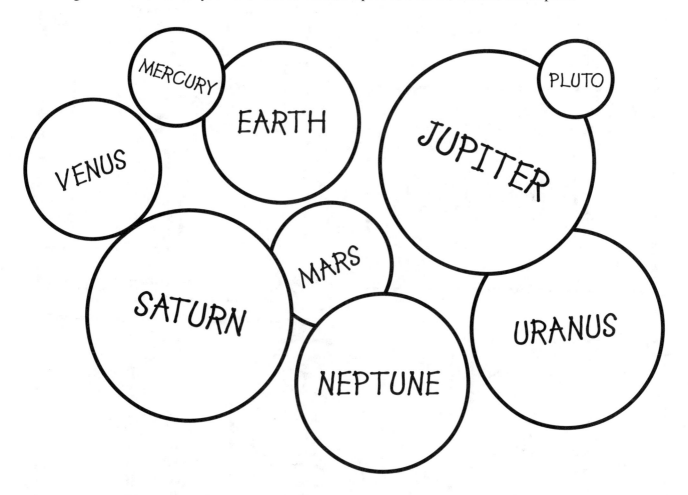

- Compare the planets: Which one is the largest? Which one is the smallest? How many planets have rings? How many planets have moons? How many planets are hot? How many are cold? How many planets are made of gas? How many planets are made of rock?

- Graph the number of nights there was a full moon, a half moon, a crescent moon, or no visible moon during the space center's use. (See Lead Ins.)

Space Travel *(cont.)*

Character Nametags

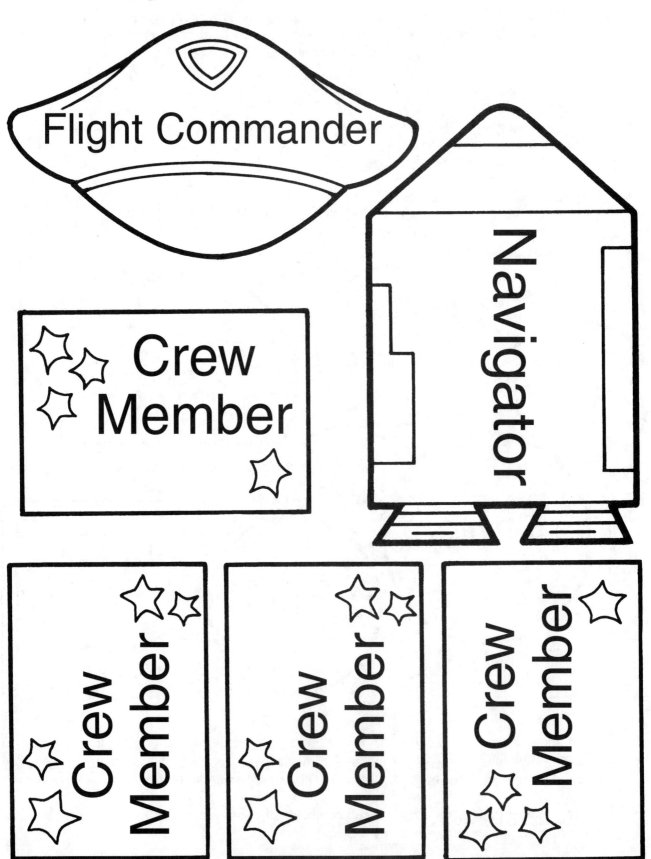

Flight Commander

Navigator

Crew Member

Crew Member

Crew Member

Crew Member

Space Travel *(cont.)*

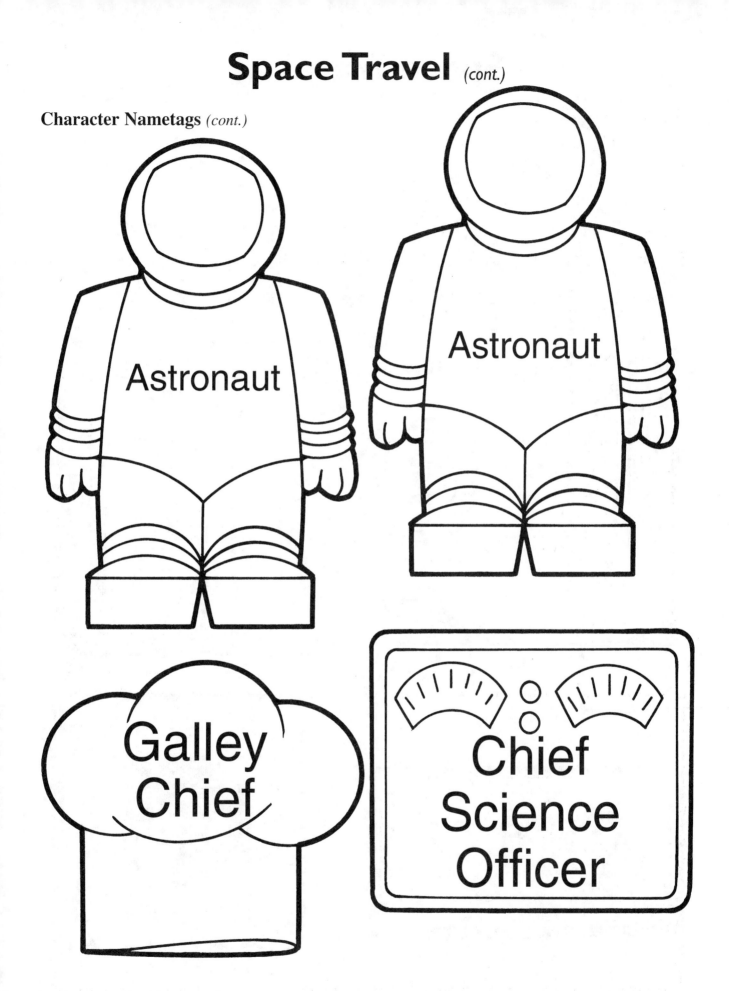

Astronaut

Astronaut

Galley Chief

Chief Science Officer

Space Travel *(cont.)*

Spaceship Gauges

Directions: Enlarge and duplicate the gauges here and on page 137 as needed to fill the spaceship.

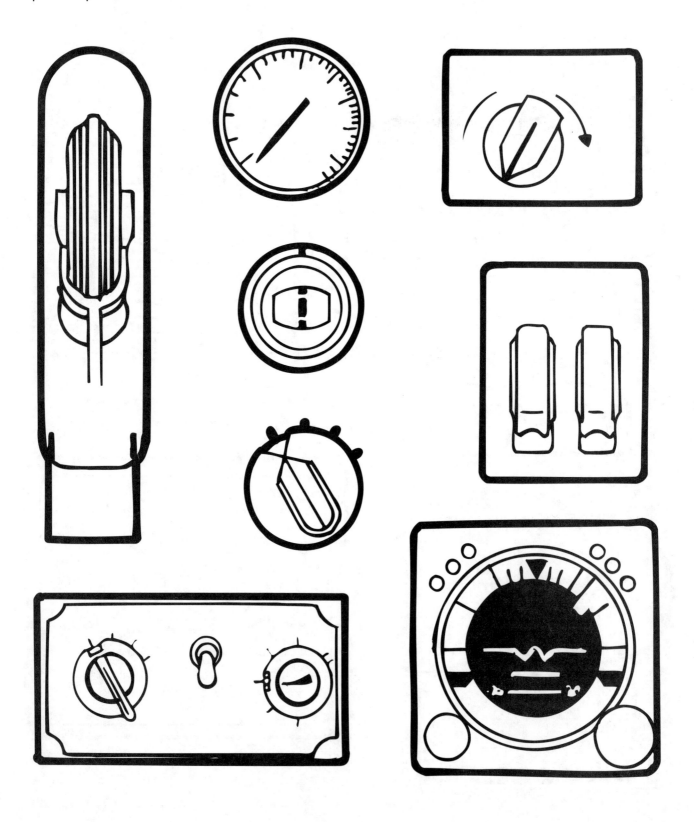

Space Travel *(cont.)*

Spaceship Gauges *(cont.)*

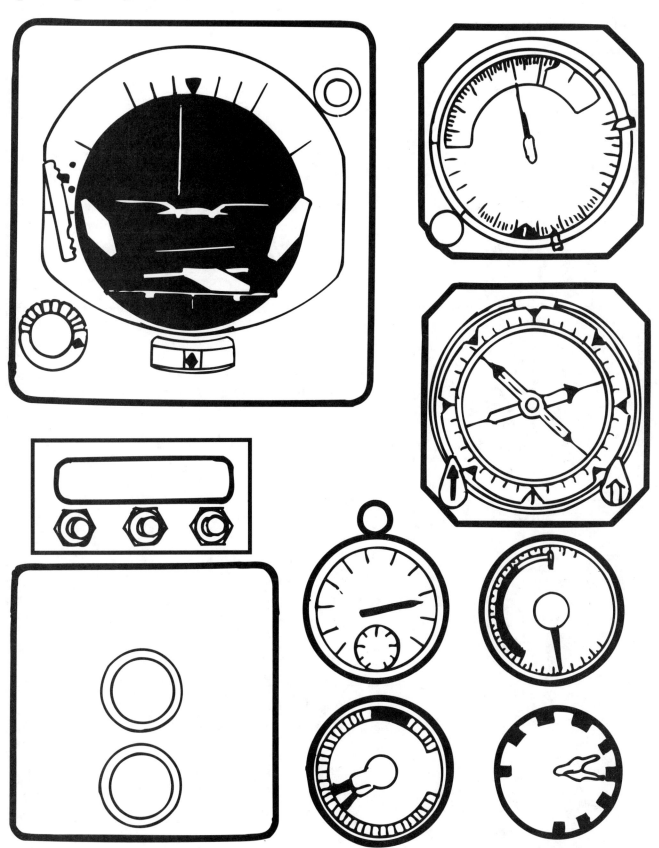

Space Travel *(cont.)*

The planets on the chart below and on page 139 are listed in their order from the sun, Mercury being the closest to the sun and Pluto, being the farthest known planet from the sun. The closer the planet is to Earth, the more information scientists have learned.

Planet Chart	
Name	**Characteristics**
Mercury	• closest planet to sun • hot, dry, no clouds, no weather • a ball of rock • no water, no life • no moons
Venus	• brightest planet • very hot, dry • covered with gas, hidden by clouds, water vapor • volcanos, earthquakes, and storms • Earth's twin • a ball of rock • no moons
Earth	• only planet with oceans • air to breathe • inhabited by people, plants, and animals • surrounded atmosphere (gases) which protects life • a ball of rock • one moon
Mars	• known as the Red Planet • cold, windy • a ball of rock, volcanoes • covered by a layer of red dust • two moons

Space Travel *(cont.)*

Planet Chart	
Name	**Characteristics**
Jupiter	• largest planet • known as the gas planet • windy • red spot • ball of gas • several moons (four large, several small)
Saturn	• large, but very light planet (it would float in water) • yellow and gray • rings made of chunks of ice and rock • 30 moons
Uranus	• 11 thin rings • bluish green color • dark, frozen surface with a metal core • small rings • five large moons and 10 small moons
Neptune	• similar in size and composition to Uranus • bluish glow • Great Dark Spot • cloudy atmosphere • foggy • rings
Pluto	• farthest planet from sun • a ball of rock • covered with ice • large moon (almost the same size as its planet)

Space Travel *(cont.)*

Counting Game Patterns

Space Travel *(cont.)*

Counting Game Patterns *(cont.)*

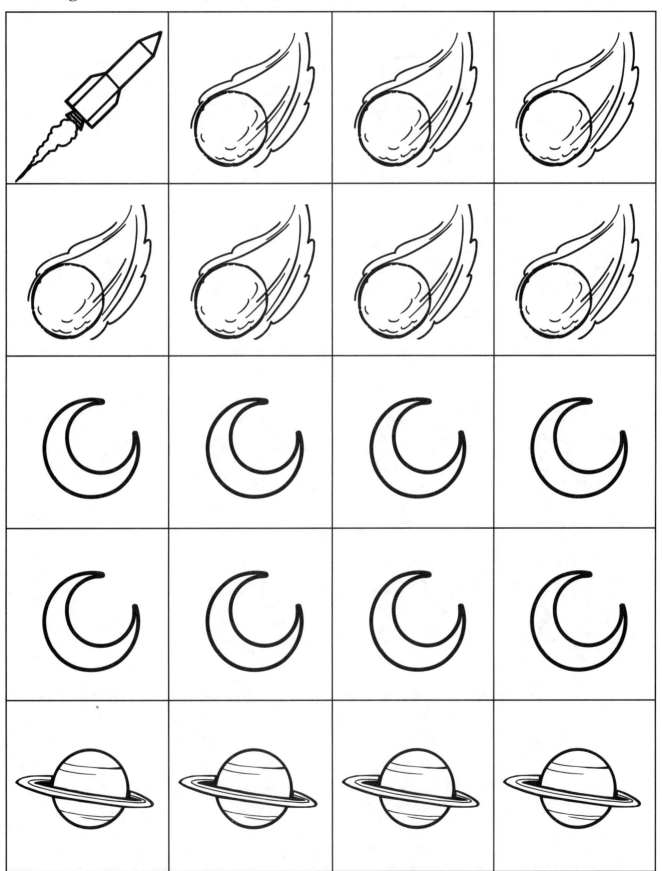

Space Travel *(cont.)*

Counting Game Patterns *(cont.)*

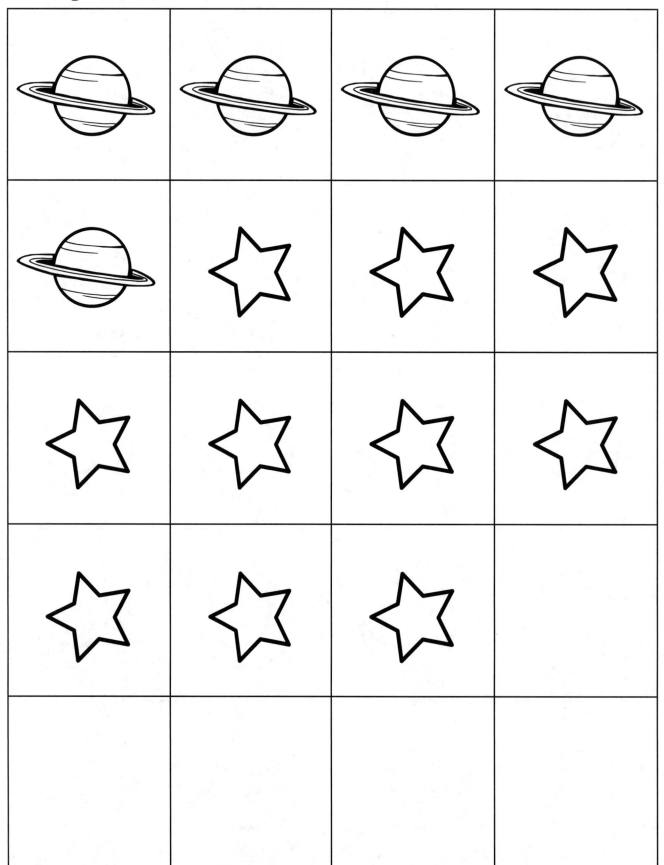

Space Travel *(cont.)*

Air Tanks

Materials

- 2L soda bottles per tank
- aluminum foil
- silver duct tape
- elastic, string, or thick yarn

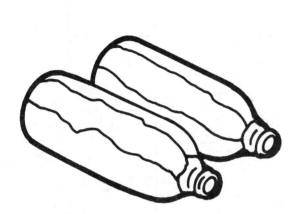

1. Cover two large, rounded plastic soda bottles with aluminum foil.

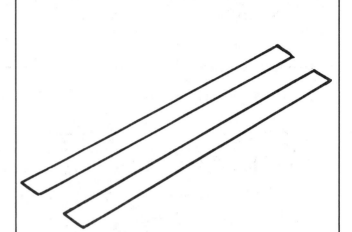

2. Lay two strips of duct tape, sticky-side up, on a table.

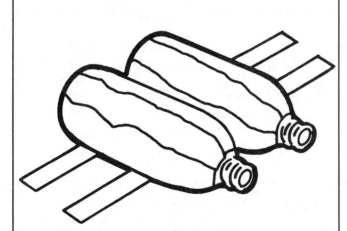

3. Place the two bottles on top of the two rows of duct tape. The necks of the bottles should be facing in the same direction.

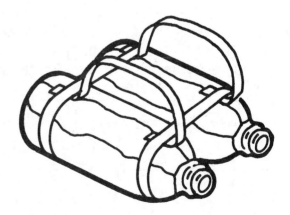

4. Create loops with the elastic to serve as shoulder straps. Use the silver duct tape to tape the covered bottles together, side-by-side, making sure to incase the shoulder straps as well.

Space Travel *(cont.)*

Space Helmets

Materials

- clean, five gallon ice cream container
- aluminum foil
- scissors
- pencil or marker

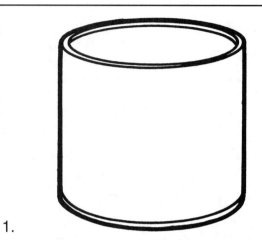

1.

The bottom of the container will become the top of the helmet.

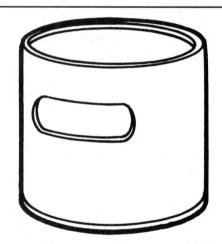

2.

Determine what style of helmet will work best for the students at the space center. Two possible options are shown above for openings. Cut the container and smooth out any rough edges. **Note:** Some students may not like feeling closed in and will prefer a larger window.

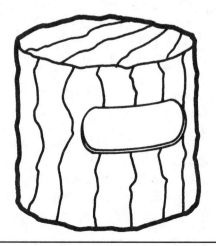

3.

Have the children try on the helmet to make certain that the "windows" are at eye level and that the helmet is comfortable. When appropriate adjustments have been made, cover the helmet with aluminum foil, leaving the "windows" open.

At the Beach

Lead Ins

- Bring a bucket of sand and a shell for each child to group time. Give the children time to examine their shells and discuss them. Then, ask where sand and shells are found. Guide the discussion toward the ocean, or if it is more appropriate, discuss a local lake. Explain that shells are protective coverings for some animals.

- Discuss beaches. Discuss the different things that can be done at a beach—swimming, beach combing, boating, sailing, scuba diving, surfing, etc. Make a class list and add to it for the duration of the dramatic play center as children submit ideas.

- Consider getting a few hermit crabs or fish for the class. Introduce them during group time, discuss their habitats and establish a routine for their care.
  Teacher Note: Hermit crabs are fascinating to watch, but they are nocturnal and sometimes need prodding during the day to come out and visit.

- Use the beach center as a springboard to introduce discussions about tide pools and the creatures that live in them—sea urchins, crabs, mussels, barnacles, sea stars, etc.

- Expand upon the beach center as time and interest allows. Introduce fish, dolphins, whales, and other animals that live in the ocean. Discuss animals that must stay in the water to live (fish, sharks, octopi, eels), animals that live in the water but breathe air (dolphins and whales), and animals that live in and out of the water (turtles, crabs, and star fish).

- Share scuba gear. Explain the purpose of fins, snorkels, scuba tanks, etc.

Safety Note: Use this center as an opportunity to discuss skin protection and the need for sun block.

At the Beach *(cont.)*

Suggested Materials for the Beach

- beach balls
- beach blankets
- beach chairs
- beach towels
- beach umbrellas
- books about tide pools and sea animals
- books about shells
- books about the ocean and other beach fronts
- children's books about the beach and sea life
- first aid kits
- fishing poles
- glitter
- old newspapers
- paint
- picnic baskets
- plastic fish and sea creatures
- sand
- sand buckets and shovels
- sand toys
- scales, all kinds
- scuba tanks
- shells
- sifters and strainers
- skim board
- snorkels
- sprinkler
- sun block
- sun hats
- sunglasses
- surfboard
- swimming pool (plastic or blow-up)
- tissue paper and streamers (blue and green)
- water table
- water toys

At the Beach (cont.)

Teacher Preparation

Since this is an outdoor dramatic play center, larger groups, or possibly the whole class, will be able to participate at the same time. For this reason, only the lifeguards and beachcombers will need nametags. The other children can be beach goers and will not necessarily need nametags.

1. Rope off a section of the outdoor play area for the beach. Add beach toys and other appropriate beach items. If a sand area is available, try to put a water table and/or plastic pool nearby.

2. Arrange an area where three or four beach towels, beach umbrellas, and beach chairs can be spread out. If no grass or sand areas are available, lay some type of padding on the play surface next to the designated water areas. (**Hint:** Go to a carpet store. Ask for a section of the foam used under carpets. Gymnastics mats and nap mats also make good padded surfaces under towels.)

3. Set up a lifeguard station or two. Labeled chairs will do. Add beach umbrellas and first aid kits. Have sun block and water available for children when the weather warrants.

4. Cut a window in a large box to use as a concession stand. Have children decorate or paint the box and use it to serve/sell snacks at the beach.

5. Set aside an area for sea creatures (plastic fish, turtles, sea stars, and crustaceans) and sea mammals (whales, dolphins). A water table or some large tubs will work. Give children opportunities to discuss where different items and animals might be found—on the shore, in a tide pool, in deep water. Post posters or pictures of tide pools, beaches, and sea animals in the classroom.

6. If your location is close to a beach area, collect samples of seaweed and kelp. Place them in a water table or large tub outside for children to examine. (**Hint:** Keep the table in the shade—the seaweed will last longer and smell less.)

7. Gather different types of sand and set up an area in the classroom for children to examine them. Ask friends and parents to bring back a bag of sand when they go on vacation. Different grades of sand can be purchased at most garden and building supply stores. Request varieties that are pre-washed.

At the Beach *(cont.)*

Teacher Preparation *(cont.)*

8. Encourage children to examine and touch the sand and to notice different colors and types of grains. Which sand is the finest grain and which is the coarsest grain? Supply magnifying glasses to look at the sand. Give children magnets to run through the sand. Some sand has iron particles in it and the magnets will pick up the particles.

9. Go to a local seafood store, seafood restaurant, or oyster bar and ask them to save shells for the class. Expand upon children's understanding of shells. Discuss other things that have shells for protection. Mention eggs, nuts, and seeds. Crabs, lobsters and snails have shells. Don't forget coconuts! If oyster, clam, or muscle shells are available, consider introducing the word bivalve and explain to children that sea animals with two matching protective shells are called bivalves.

10. Create a fishing game using the patterns and directions on page 156. Use the activity to work on fine and gross motor skill development or label the fish to work on alphabet letters, words, numbers or math facts.

11. Plan a special "Day at the Beach" or a day of the week for the duration of the center when the children will be allowed to wear bathing suits and play in small pools or a sprinkler. Send home a letter (page 157) requesting that children bring bathing suits, sunscreen, bag lunches, and towels to school on a designated day.

12. Create an Undersea World. Use a tent, a sun awning (like the ones brought to children's sporting events), or the underside of a climbing structure. Cut streamers to represent seaweed and kelp and hang it from the top of the tent or the underside of the structure. Suspend fish and other sea creatures. String strands of Styrofoam packing material to simulate strands of octopus eggs. Add the stuffed fish the children make.

13. Make scuba tanks (see Air Tanks, page 143) and let the children take turns pretending to be scuba divers swimming around. Add masks and fins for added interest.

14. Invite a lifeguard or a park ranger to visit the class to share what he or she does each day to protect the beach, sea life, and the people who visit the beach.

15. Invite a scuba diver or surfer to come to class to share his or her experiences.

At the Beach (cont.)

Student Preparation

1. Use two long strips of bulletin-board paper to make a beach scene mural. Paint one strip to resemble sand. Add some salt to tan or light brown tempera paint to change its texture or cover the bulletin-board paper with glue (mixed with brown paint) and sprinkle sand over it. When the sand part of the mural dries, glue shells, seaweed (or green, brown, and red cutouts of seaweed), and cutouts of pails, shovels, and sand toys to it.

   The second strip of the mural will be the water. Add some salt to the blue paint. The salt will make the mural sparkle when it dries. Paint the water different shades of blue. Use dark blue paint on the top of the paper. Then, add some white paint to the blue paint to lighten the color. Finish the bulletin-board paper with the lighter paint.

   Teacher Note: When hanging the children's beach mural, explain that the deeper water will be a darker shade. Connect the water portion of the mural to the sand portion. The dark water will be on the top (horizon) and the shallow, lighter colored water will be touching the sand. Mention to the children that, when they look at the mural, they should imagine that they are standing on the sand looking out toward the horizon and the deeper water.

2. Add shells to the shoreline and other sea creatures to the water. Patterns for shells are available on pages 152–154 and tide pool creatures on page 155. These can be traced, colored, and cut out, or precut on construction paper and added to the mural. Draw beach items, as well, or add cutouts from magazines. Cover sea star shapes with glue and birdseed or wood shavings for a textured effect.

3. Make a sign that says, "This way to the beach!" Decorate it with pictures cut out from a magazines, photographs, and cutout patterns.

4. Paint a large box cut out to serve as a beach concession stand. Later, take turns "selling" snack from the stand.

5. Make "sandpaper" samples by gluing some of each available type of sand to large paper letters, S–A–N–D. Display the sand letters in the beach area or the classroom.

6. Sort a shell collection. Decide which shells are bivalves.

7. Look at pictures of tide pools and then create them in the sand. Dig holes and add rocks. Later fill the holes in the sand with shells, sea stars, seaweed, crabs, etc. Use some of the shell collection, and add plastic sea animals. Barnacles can easily be made by cutting individual sections of paper egg cartons, poking holes in them and pushing a bit of tissue paper up through the holes.

8. Help make the Undersea World. Cut out large fish patterns. Make two of each pattern and paint them. Add glitter to the paint as it dries. When the paint is completely dry, staple around the edges of the fish, leaving an opening to stuff newspaper strips through.

At the Beach *(cont.)*

Vocabulary Building

barnacles	coastline	grain	oyster	seaside	spiral
beach	concession stand	horizon	rough	seaweed	triton
beachcomber	conch	kelp	scallop	shell	urchin
bivalve	cone	lakeside	scuba diver	shore	waves
clam	fins	lifeguard	sea star	shoreline	
coarse	fine	mussel	seashore	snorkel	

Literacy Component

- Design a sand castle using damp sand and different sized cups and containers. Later, dictate a story about life in the castle mentioning the different sections created.
- Draw spirals similar to the inside of conch, snail, or nautilus shells using patterns on page 154.
- Discuss the word *bivalve* and explain that it means two valves, just as bicycle means a bike with two wheels. Trace around different bivalve shells. Hold the shell in the middle with one hand and hold the pencil or crayon with the other hand. Cut out two patterns, staple them together, and add a pearl (bead) or animal drawing to the inside.
- Describe walking on a sandy beach. If a sand area is not available, take turns stepping barefoot into a tub of sand. Make lists of descriptive words—coarse, fine, grainy, squishy, etc.
- Use "the beach" to work on spatial concepts. (Fish swim *in* the water. Boats float *on* the water.)
- Read books about tide pools and the seashore. See how many creatures can be listed that inhabit the two areas of the beach. Include the animals on page 155.
- Begin a list of animals that have shells for protection and animals that have internal skeletons to protect their vital organs. (**Note:** Turtles and tortoises are unique. They have the double protection of shells and skeletons.)
- Learn the differences between fish and sea mammals.

Numeracy Component

- Sort shells from the shell collection by color, size, or shape. Count the shells in each set.
- Count and sort the sea animals in the class collection or a series of pictures. Consider dividing the groups into animals that live on the shore versus those that live in the water or animals with fins versus those with legs or claws.
- Arrange the sea animal collection by size. Determine which sea animals are the largest in real life.
- Bivalves are animals protected by pairs of matching shells. What other pairs of things can be found in the beach dramatic play center? Encourage each participant to find a pair of items (any kind) to share.
- Use the sea life collection or pictures to sort. Create a Venn diagram to divide fish and mammals or animals with shells and those without shells.
- Compare the weight of a cup of wet sand and a cup of dry sand. Discuss which is heavier and why. What happens to the wet sand when it dries? Does it weigh the same amount? What else can be weighed in the beach center?
- Use the fishing poles (page 156). See how many fish can be caught in a specified amount of time.
- Look at pictures of sea stars. Count the arms on each one. How many arms do most sea stars have? (five)
- Make sea urchins. Roll balls of play dough or clay and stick a predetermined number of toothpicks or craft sticks into them. Use the number cards (Appendix, pages 242–244) to specify the number of legs for the sea urchins being made.

At the Beach *(cont.)*

Character Nametags

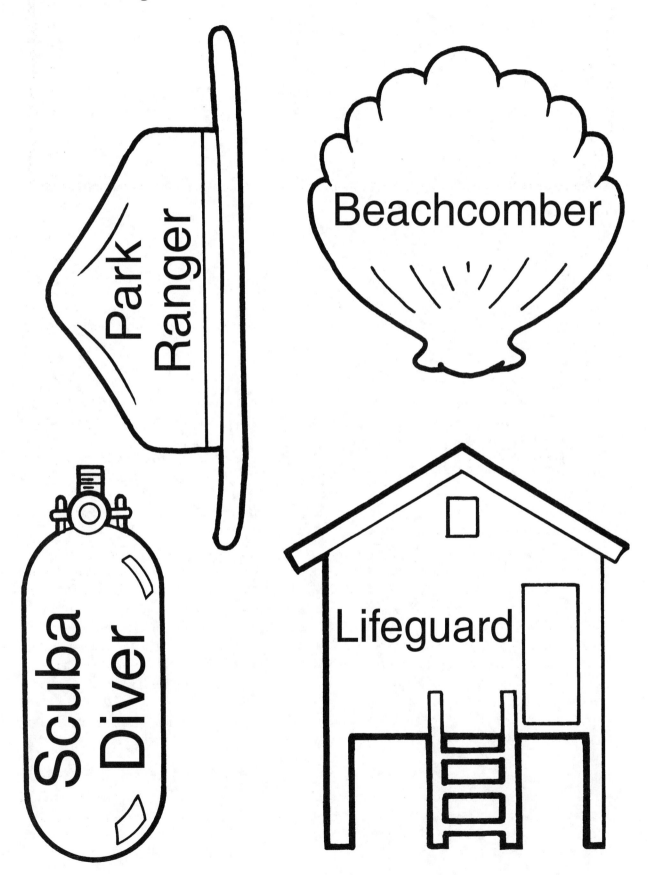

At the Beach *(cont.)*

Shells

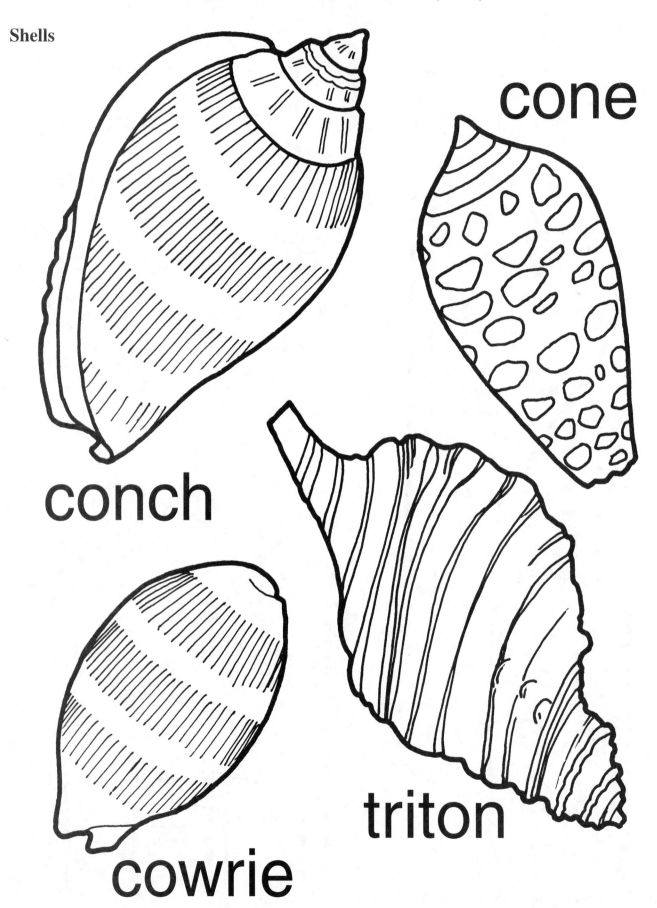

cone

conch

cowrie

triton

At the Beach *(cont.)*

Shells *(cont.)*

oyster

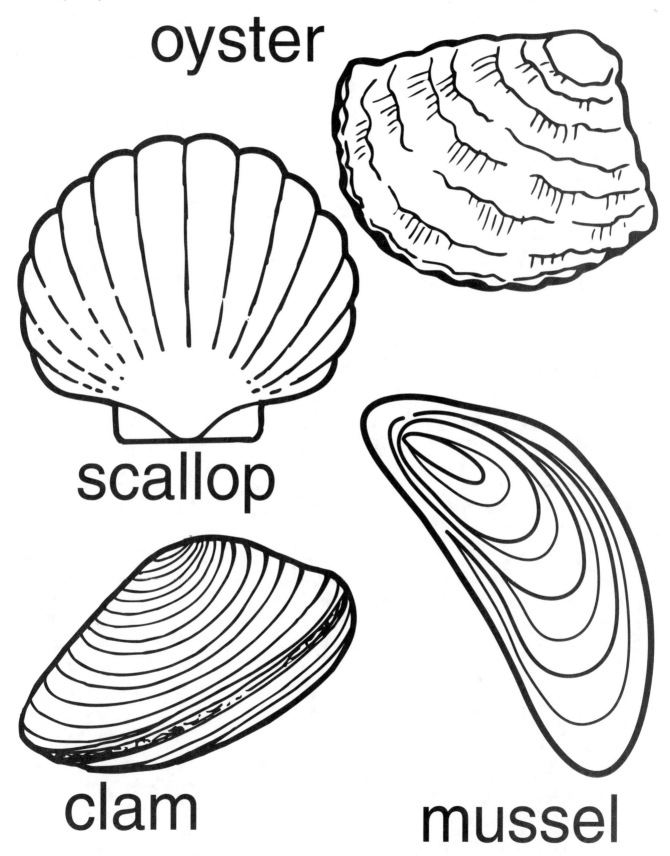

scallop

clam

mussel

At the Beach *(cont.)*

Spiral Shell

Trace the spiral on the shell.

Nautilus

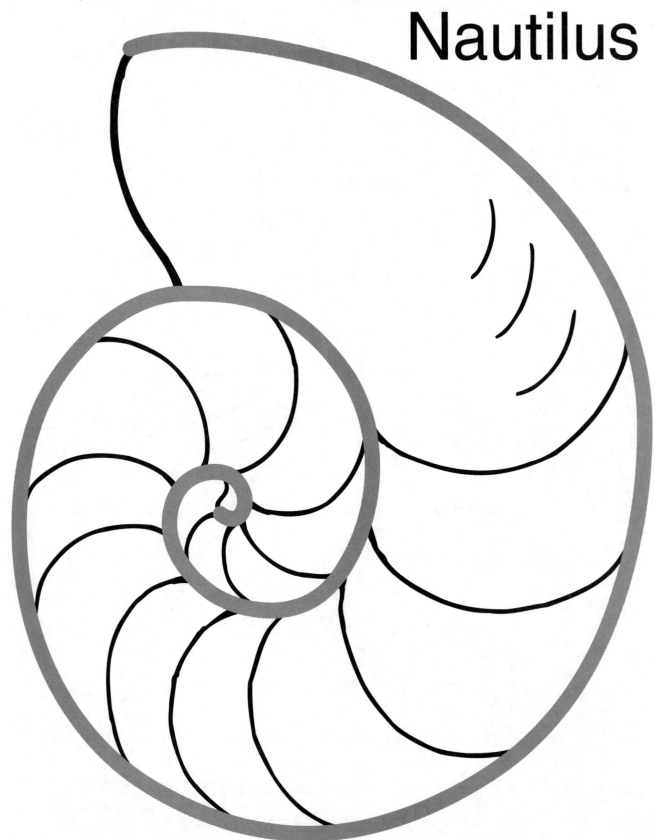

At the Beach (cont.)

Tide Pool Creatures

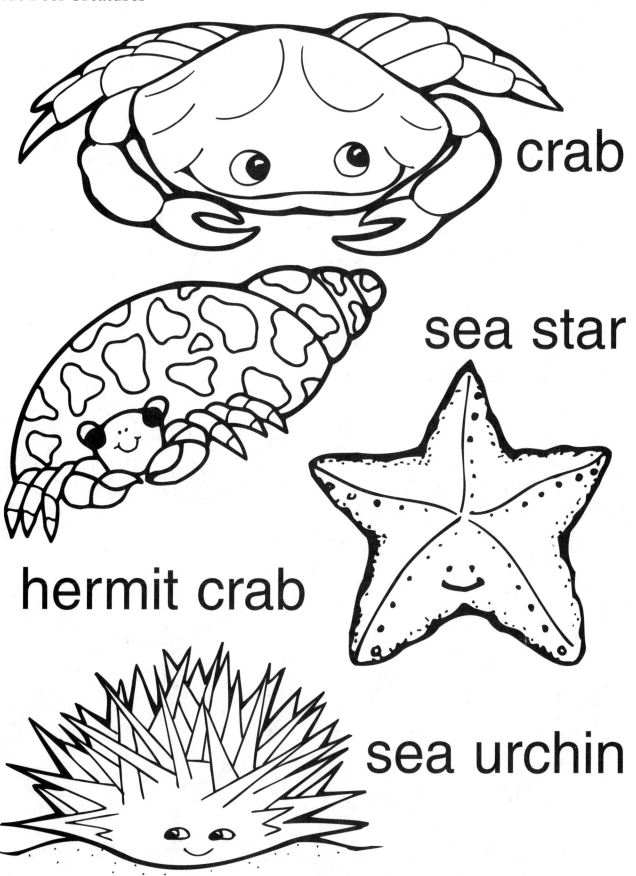

crab

sea star

hermit crab

sea urchin

At the Beach *(cont.)*

Materials

- 18" (45 cm) dowel
- magnet
- fish patterns (Enlarge patterns to suit needs.)
- 18" (45 cm) string or thick yarn
- paper clips

Directions

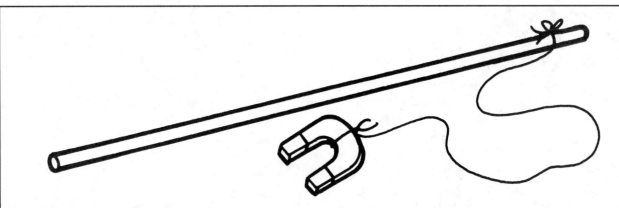

1. Tie or tape the string to one end of the dowel. Attach the magnet to the other end of the string.

2. Attach paper clips to each fish.

At the Beach (cont.)

Date:_____

Dear Parents,

Now that the weather is so warm, we have set up one of our famous literacy centers outside. It is called "At the Beach." We would like to ask that the children bring bathing suits, sun screen, a bag lunch, and a towel on

_____.

We will have water play and a picnic lunch outside and want to make it a real day at the beach.

Thank you,

_____

Teacher

Digging for Dinosaurs

Lead Ins

- Bring a few plastic dinosaurs or illustrations of dinosaurs to group time and ask if the children can identify them. Most young children are quite knowledgeable about dinosaurs. Once they have had time to share what they know, ask them how we know so much about dinosaurs. Explain that certain scientists, called "paleontologists" learn about them by studying the dinosaur bones, eggs, and footprints (fossils) that have been discovered over the years.

- Ask a butcher to save a large bone for a class presentation. Scrub it clean and soak the bone in bleach water. Bury the clean, bleached bone in a tub of sand. Arrange the bone so that it is slightly protruding from the sand. Bring the prepared tub to group time and tell the children that they are going to be paleontologists at a digging site. Explain that you are going to demonstrate how a paleontologist excavates a dinosaur bone at a "dig." Ask the children to look closely at the sand and tell what they see. (See illustration.)

- Encourage the children to describe the sand, the tub, and anything else they notice. When the bone is spotted, congratulate the children on their find. Explain that you will demonstrate how a paleontologist might approach this important find. First, scoop away the surrounding sand using a spoon or small shovel. Next, brush away the sand covering the bone. When the bone has been uncovered, carefully lift it out and place it on a clean surface.

- As a group, spend some time describing the discovery (bone), noting its shape and colors. Write down descriptive words. Measure and weigh the bone. Encourage the children to draw pictures of the bone. Explain that note-taking is part of a scientific dig like the ones they will experience in the Digging for Dinosaurs center.

Digging for Dinosaurs (cont.)

Suggested Materials for Digging for Dinosaurs

- backpacks or satchels
- bandanas
- bones
- books about archeology, dinosaurs, and artifacts
- brushes (old toothbrushes, paint brushes, and scrub brushes)
- camera
- clear plastic containers
- clipboards
- dinosaur skeleton models
- dinosaur posters and pictures
- dinosaurs
- feather dusters
- hats with protective brims
- magnifying glasses
- painters caps
- pith helmets
- plastic eggs
- polished stones
- rope or plastic tape
- rulers
- sand
- scales
- sifters
- small shovels
- spoons
- strainers
- string
- tarp

Digging for Dinosaurs *(cont.)*

Teacher Preparation

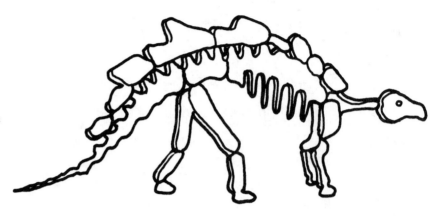

1. The first step in creating an archeological dig site is finding an appropriate location. A sand box or dirt area suitable for digging is the optimal choice. If this is not possible, use a sand table or large tubs filled with sand or dirt. Mark the area with rope or plastic tape (from a hardware or garden supply store) and mark it with signs made by the children.

2. Decide what type of dig will start the discovery. One exciting option is to purchase a dinosaur skeleton kit. These kits are usually made of balsa wood pieces and can be purchased in hobby shops, craft stores, or toy stores. The "bones" from the kit can be buried separately and then assembled once all the pieces have been found. These balsa wood skeleton kits are particularly good when more than one team will be digging, since new groups of bones can be dug up by each group and then assembled later by the whole class. Another option is to bury a number of bones from the butcher and pretend that they are dinosaur bones. Using real bones is particularly effective when a lot of weighing and measuring is planned. Add some fossils, polished stones, and other items of interest to the dig site to make things interesting.

3. Use string to create a grid over the sand and buried items. Divide the area into quadrants, six sections or more, depending on the allotted space. (See illustration.)

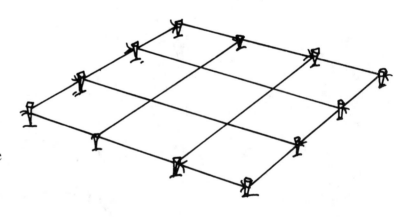

4. Make replicas of the grid on bulletin-board paper. Each team should have a dig site. If only one site is feasible, establish a schedule for each team to work the site. Each member of the archeological team can be assigned a section of the grid.

5. Plan attire for the paleontologists. Try different colored bandanas for the different positions on the excavation team. Also use hats or pith helmets. Use backpacks to carry the different tools necessary.

Digging for Dinosaurs (cont.)

Teacher Preparation (cont.)

6. Make labels for the site and nametags for the team (pages 165–166). All members of the team can be called paleontologists or each member can have a title based on a specific job. Possibilities include the following:

   Digger—moves sand or earth away from the object without touching the object.

   Sifter—sifts through the sand or earth that has been moved.
   Note: Try to have some small, special rocks, bits of polished beach glass, arrowheads, or other items that sifters can discover.

   Brusher—brushes away sand or earth from the partially excavated item before it is removed from the dig site.

   Site Foreman—is in charge of the equipment. The site foreman makes certain that workers are careful at the site.

   Recorder—records each artifact as it is discovered. A recorder can draw, weigh, and/or measure the artifact.

   Determine ahead of time the number of paleontologists, diggers, sifters, site foreman, and recorders each dig site can accommodate and make nametags to suit.

7. Introduce the grid map of the digging site during a group time or special outside group time. Explain that you will need to take turns so each person can work carefully without being crowded. Remind the children that as paleontologists they need to make sure that they do not step on an artifact while they are working. Have children sign up in a section of the grid map when it is their turn. Remind the children that it is important to treat the discoveries gently.

8. Establish an area to display and catalog the excavated items. Have scales, measurement tools, graph and drawing paper, and writing and drawing implements. If appropriate, make copies of the Excavation Log on page 167. Attach the logs to clipboards for each team. If a balsa wood skeleton is buried, have an area set aside for reconstruction once all of the bones have been discovered.

9. Document the dig. Take pictures of the site before excavation, the paleontologists at work, and the discoveries. Photograph children weighing, measuring, and illustrating their finds. Incorporate the pictures into a class book. (See Literacy Component, page 163.)

10. If a balsa wood skeleton is created, have a grand unveiling picnic near the dig site at the end of the Digging for Dinosaurs center.

11. If possible, plan a trip to a museum to view actual dinosaur skeletons or have a paleontologist or archeologist visit your site.

Digging for Dinosaurs *(cont.)*

Student Preparation

1. Name the site. Create signs for the digging site on large, dinosaur-shaped pieces of paper. Decorate the signs with pictures or stampings of dinosaurs, bones, and excavating tools.

2. Sort tools into containers or backpacks. Count the tools in each container. Label each container with the name and the number of tools that it holds. Have the site foreman count and sort the tools at the end of each session.

3. Shape bones and other artifacts out of clay or cover small plastic dinosaurs with lumps of hardening clay to form eggs (with baby dinosaurs inside). Let the creations harden and use them later in the dig sites.

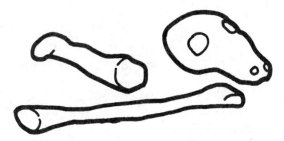

4. Draw pictures of the dig site once it has been established. Make additional drawings once the excavations are underway.

5. Create a large mural for the classroom. Paint mountains, a lake or river, the sky, and a bright sun. Draw or cut out pictures of dinosaurs to add to the mural. Embellish the scene with clouds made of cotton balls, tissue paper flowers, and construction paper trees.

Vocabulary Building

dig	gentle	sifter
claws	illustrate	site
excavate	measure	skeleton
extinct	paleontologist	skull
fossil	record (verb)	strainer
fragile	scientist	

Dinosaur Names

Ankylosaurus	Diplodocus	Styracosaurus
Apatosaurus (Brontosaurus)	Iguanodon	Triceratops
Brachiosaurus	Pteranodon	Tyrannosaurus Rex
Dimetrodon	Pterodactl	
	Stegosaurus	

Note: List additional dinosaurs included in the study.

Digging for Dinosaurs *(cont.)*

Literacy Component

- Make a list of dinosaur names. Decorate the classroom and the dig site with posters and pictures of dinosaurs. Make labels and (have the children) attach the appropriate label to each dinosaur picture. Continue this practice as more pictures are added.

- Read the list of dinosaur names together in class. Clap out the syllables for each dinosaur. Which dinosaur name has the most syllables? Which dinosaur names end the same (-saurus, odon)?

- Learn more about dinosaurs. Find out which ones were carnivores (meat eaters) and which were herbivores (plant eaters). Make a chart with the findings.

- Plant eaters with short teeth for grinding included horned dinosaurs (Triceratops), long-necked dinosaurs (Apatosaurus, Diplodocus), armored dinosaurs (Stegosaurus, Iguanodon, Anklosaurus), and duck-billed dinosaurs (Parasaurolophus). Tyrannosaurus Rex had sharp, pointed teeth and was a meat eater. Pteranodons flew over the water and caught fish to eat.

- Enlarge the Dinosaur Footprint on page 168. Cut out the footprint and use it as a frame for dictated stories about dinosaurs or make copies and create a classroom journal detailing an excavation. Create a cover in the same shape, using construction paper.

- Make two laminated sets of dinosaur cards (pages 169–170). Use them in a literacy center to play matching games. Make more sets of the cards for patterning games.

- Design dinosaurs using cardboard shapes, clay or play dough. Add beans, rice, or pasta details. (See illustration.) When the dinosaurs are completed, take turns talking about the creations. Allow time to write or dictate descriptions of these dinosaurs. Encourage discussions about habitats, food, color, protective features, and size.

- Tell or dictate stories describing a day in the life of a favorite dinosaur.

- Take turns describing different dinosaurs. Mimic their actions. Try to get others to guess which dinosaur is being described.

Digging for Dinosaurs (cont.)

Numeracy Component

- Count and log in artifacts as they are excavated. Use the Excavation Log on page 167 or draw pictures of the artifacts on copies of the footprint pattern on page 168.

- Measure items as they are excavated. Compare the lengths of different bones. Imagine how long real dinosaurs might have been. Get a long rope or a ball of twine and take it outside to demonstrate approximate lengths of different dinosaurs. Use the list below as a guide.

- Weigh bones as they are excavated. Compare the weights of the different bones. Arrange the bones by weight. Put the heaviest at one end of the display and the lightest bone at the other end. Continually adjust the display as new bones are uncovered.

- Sort the bones. How many are curved and how many are straight? How many are longer or shorter than a specific classroom object (eraser, crayon, etc.)?

- Use the Dinosaur Footprint on page 168 as a nonstandard measurement tool. (The footprint can be enlarged to suit.)

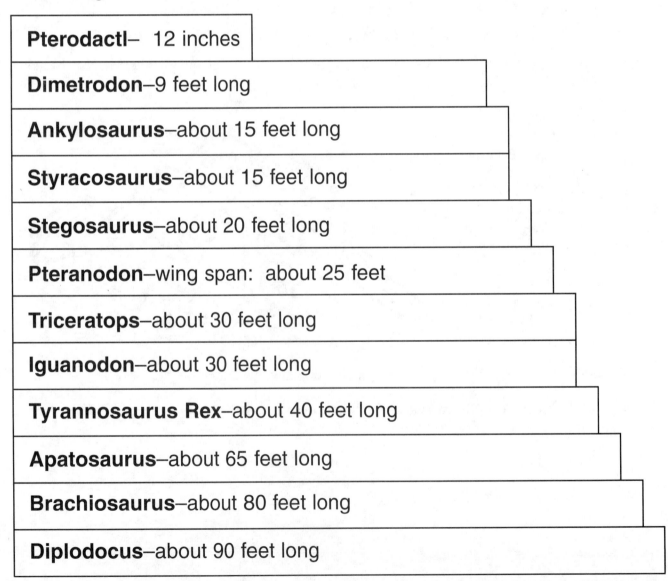

Pterodactl– 12 inches

Dimetrodon–9 feet long

Ankylosaurus–about 15 feet long

Styracosaurus–about 15 feet long

Stegosaurus–about 20 feet long

Pteranodon–wing span: about 25 feet

Triceratops–about 30 feet long

Iguanodon–about 30 feet long

Tyrannosaurus Rex–about 40 feet long

Apatosaurus–about 65 feet long

Brachiosaurus–about 80 feet long

Diplodocus–about 90 feet long

Digging for Dinosaurs *(cont.)*

Character Nametags

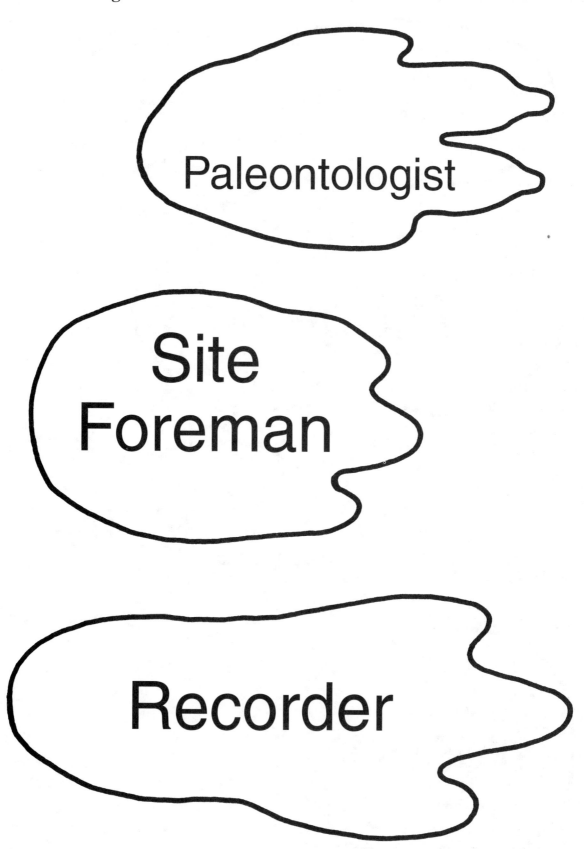

Paleontologist

Site Foreman

Recorder

Digging for Dinosaurs (cont.)

Character Nametags (cont.)

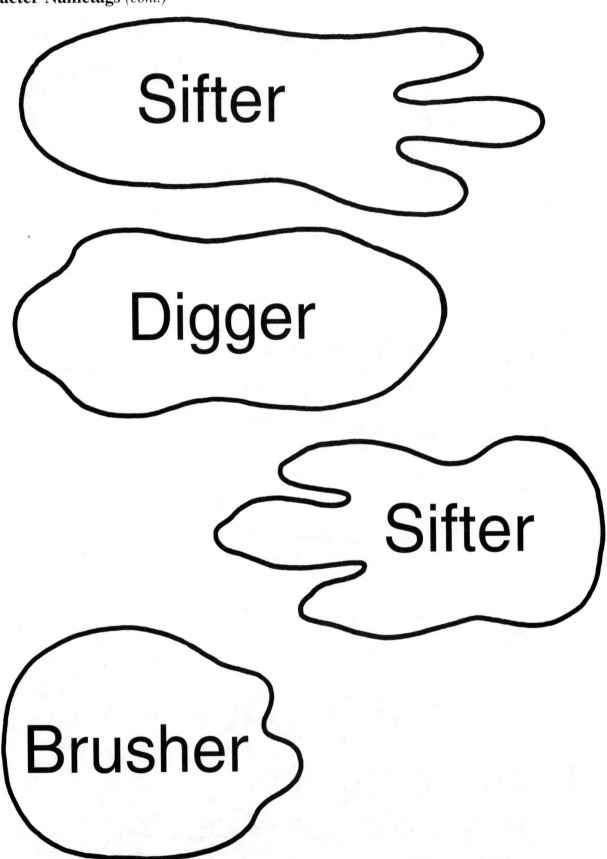

Sifter

Digger

Sifter

Brusher

Digging for Dinosaurs (cont.)

Today we found a _____.
This is a picture of our find.

Today we found a _____.
This is a picture of our find.

Digging for Dinosaurs (cont.)

Dinosaur Footprint

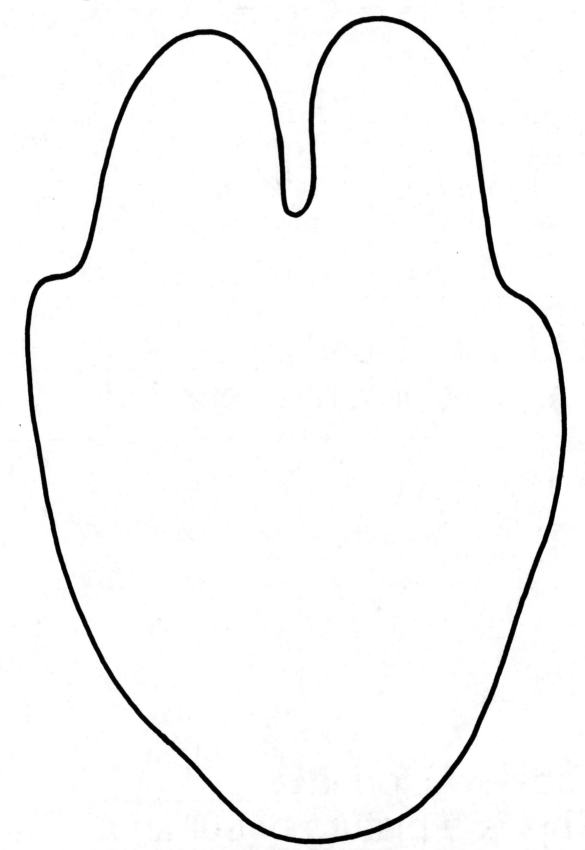

168

Digging for Dinosaurs *(cont.)*

Dinosaur Cards

Ankylosaurus

Dimetrodon

Apatosaurus

Diplodocus

Brachiosaurus

Iguanodon

Digging for Dinosaurs (cont.)

Dinosaur Cards (cont.)

Pteranodon

Styracosaurus

Pterodactl

Triceratops

Stegosaurus

Tyrannosaurus Rex

Drive-Thru Restaurant

Lead Ins

- Bring a breakfast or lunch container from a drive-thru restaurant to school. Ask what it is and where it came from. How do they know? Have they been to that restaurant or do they recognize the logo on the container?

- Take a poll of the drive-thru restaurants children have gone to with their families. List or graph the restaurants to see which is the drive-thru most often frequented by the children with their families.

- Ask the children who have gone to a drive-thru to describe the process. Where do you order the food? How do you get your food after it is ordered? Where do you eat the food? Do you get other things with the food (prizes, games)?

- Create a Venn diagram with the children. Compare a "sit-down" restaurant with a drive-thru restaurant. Which things are the same in both types of restaurants? Which things are different? Discuss bags and wrappers versus plates and the different kinds of silverware, indoor/outdoor seating, food servers (waiters and waitresses) versus counter people, etc.

Suggested Materials for the Drive-thru Restaurant

- "to go" containers
- aprons
- baseball caps
- bikes, tricycles, and other playground vehicles
- boxes (to make cars, vans, and other vehicles)
- cash registers
- chef's hats
- food items (plastic)
- headsets
- large boxes (to make drive-up windows)
- menus
- money (page 246–247)
- paper cups with matching lids
- small paper bags
- snack items
- straws
- vests
- Talk to managers at different restaurants. Often, they will make supply donations to a class project. Try to get hats, serving items, children's place mats (the ones with games, riddles, and activities on them), etc.

Drive-Thru Restaurant (cont.)

Teacher Preparation

1. Set up a shelf or counter for the cooking/food prep area, a table or two for patrons, the drive-thru window, and an area for cashiers. You may wish to have a "Walk-up" window as well.

2. Make labels for the restaurant and the service windows and nametags for the participants. Determine ahead of time the number of cooks, patrons, counter persons, window attendants, etc. that your restaurant can accommodate and make copies to suit. Add a capacity card to the entrance of the kitchen area. Review the labels and character nametags during group time.

3. Determine a maximum number of participants for the servers and place a number card under the restaurant sign to remind the children. Number cards can be found in the Appendix on pages 242–244. The rest of the class can be customers.

4. Gather or create uniform items to go with the character nametags. Paper hats, vests, and aprons will work well for the employees. A headset could be used for the person taking orders.

5. Work with the children to develop a list of items for sale. This list can change from week to week to accommodate different favorite restaurants. Create menus. Add food items from the classroom, the food cards on pages 178–179, or use pictures from magazines or drawings.

6. Determine a price list and create appropriate money. See pages 246–247 in the Appendix. **Teacher Note:** This drive-thru window may become a regular feature during snack time and is a great way for introducing advanced money concepts. Simply raise the prices as children's number concept skills improve.

7. Prepare the service window. Cut a large rectangle out of the top half of a box. If the box will sit on an outdoor table, plan on having a chair behind it. If it is a large (appliance) box for more than one counter person, cut the "window" to the appropriate height for the workers. After the children have decorated the box, arrange chairs and a small table inside to hold the food and cash register. It is probably a good idea to cut out the bottom two thirds of the back of the appliance box for easy exit and entry.

8. You want to have a second smaller box where children "drive up" and place their orders. In this case, you will need an additional server to take the orders and run them inside.

9. The drive-thru restaurant is a great treat for children. Use it for snack time. Simply place the snack of the day in cups, coffee filters, or small bags and bring it outside. Give each child a ticket, a token, or play money. If there is more than one choice, let each child place his or her order, pay, and take the chosen snack to a nearby "dining area."

10. Create matching games or memory games for an indoor extension to the center. Use the food card pictures on pages 178–180.

11. Plan a field trip to a local drive-thru during the use of the center or have a parent order for the class and bring it back for a special treat.

Drive-Thru Restaurant *(cont.)*

Student Preparation

1. Vote on a name for the drive-thru restaurant and make a sign for it. Create a logo and a color scheme. Add pictures from advertisements and/or menus from different foods that are served in the restaurant.

2. Gather wallets, purses, checkbooks, etc. Make the appropriate money based on the established price list.

3. Make cars to go to the drive-thru restaurant. Cut off the top of the box (or use the bottom of a copy paper box) and make a large hole in the bottom. The box should be able to be worn around the mid-section. Add "suspenders" using twine, ribbon or elastic. Paint the vehicle. Use larger boxes to make larger cars, vans, etc. Add headlights, grills, wheels, and other details. (See illustration and cover photo.)

4. Decorate the service window (box). Glue flyers, menus, and pictures of food items to the outside. Set aside a large area on the box for an enlarged price list.

5. Practice taking and preparing orders.

6. Play the food card games. (See Teacher Preparation, step 10.)

Vocabulary Building

bucket	order
cooks	order takers
counter persons	patrons
customers	service
double	single
drive-in	small
fast food	super-size
large	take-out
medium	window attendants
menu	

Drive-Thru Restaurant *(cont.)*

Literacy Component

- Practice oral communication skills, placing orders, listening to orders, and correctly filling orders.

- Practice manners—asking politely and saying thank you, waiting in line, etc.

- Use the picture menus to place and fill orders. Circle the items requested.

- Use the food cards to create patterns or to match pre-made pattern strips. (See example.)

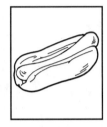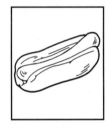

- Make a list of the different ways drive-thru restaurant food is packaged. Include paper wrappings, bags, Styrofoam containers, cardboard boxes, buckets, etc.

- Play memory games with the food cards. Make two sets of cards and laminate them, if possible. Mix up the two sets of cards and lay them face down. Take turns flipping over two cards and trying to find a match. If the player finds a match, he or she keeps the pair of cards and continues the game, turning over two more cards. When the two cards flipped over do not match, they are turned back over (in the same spot) and it is the next player's turn. Continue until all the pairs of food cards have been matched.

- Play a variation of "Go Fish" using two laminated sets of the food cards. Deal four or five cards to each player. Spread out the remaining cards, facedown, in front of the players. This will be the "fish pond." Have the players take any pairs from their cards and place them in front of them. Then, each player takes a turn asking for matches to his or her remaining cards. For example, "Do you have any hamburgers?" If the player who was asked has the requested card, the card is turned over and the player who asked gets another turn. If the card is not available from the player asked, it is the next player's turn. Play continues until all the food cards have been matched.

Numeracy Component

- Make money to match the menu prices. Practice paying for the item desired. For young children, equate one item with one piece of money. When appropriate, encourage the children to order and pay for more than one item at a time.

- Make change for large bills when customers pay for their meals.

- Discuss sizes in relation to placing orders at a drive-thru restaurant. Use play dough to make different menu items. Roll out hamburger patties. Make a single burger, a double, and a triple hamburger or label a group of small fast food boxes for different numbers of chicken strips. Have the children fill the cardboard fast food boxes with play dough chicken pieces.

- Use the sequencing cards on page 180 to discuss the following size concepts—small, medium, large, super-sized; 3 pieces, 6 pieces, 9 pieces, 12 pieces; single, double, triple.

Drive-Thru Restaurant (cont.)

Character Nametags

Cook

Counter Person

Manager

Drive-Thru Restaurant (cont.)

Character Nametags (cont.)

Drive-Thru Restaurant (cont.)

Menu

cheeseburger

milk shake

hamburger

nachos

hot dog

soda

French fries

chicken

ice-cream cone

taco

Drive-Thru Restaurant *(cont.)*

Food Cards

cheeseburger

hamburger

double cheeseburger

hot dog

French fries

taco

Drive-Thru Restaurant *(cont.)*

bucket of chicken

milk shake

chicken pieces

nachos

ice-cream cone

soda

Drive-Thru Restaurant *(cont.)*

Food Sizes (Sequencing Cards)

drink	drink	drink	drink
small	medium	large	super-size

chicken	chicken	chicken	chicken
3 pieces	6 pieces	9 pieces	12 pieces

burger	burger	burger
single	double	triple

Gas Station

Lead Ins

- During a snack or lunch period, ask children why they eat food. Guide them to recognize that food is fuel for their bodies. Explain that they need food to help their bodies grow and move. Food gives us energy. Ask, "Does a car eat food?" When the chuckles subside, ask how cars run? Someone's parent is bound to have run out of gas and the discussion should get rolling. Take time to mention the types of gas different vehicles use (just as people eat different foods). Make a list of different types of gas—regular, supreme, diesel, etc.

- Ask who has been to a gas station. What kinds of gas stations are common in the area? Do they strictly sell gas? Do they sell food or car supplies? Can you get your car fixed or washed there? Make a chart or graph indicating the types of gas stations they are most familiar with or the one they like the best. Use the markers below to label the chart.

- Discuss the different things that people do at a gas station to take care of their vehicles—put air in the tires, check water in the radiator, clean the windshield, check the oil, etc.

- Brainstorm a list of workers in the gas station. You may wish to discuss the "gas stations of old" where the attendants checked the oil, washed the windows, and pumped the gas for customers. (Adjust the character nametags offered in this section and in the Appendix to suit this list.)

- Introduce stories and informational books about cars, trucks, and service stations.

Graph Markers

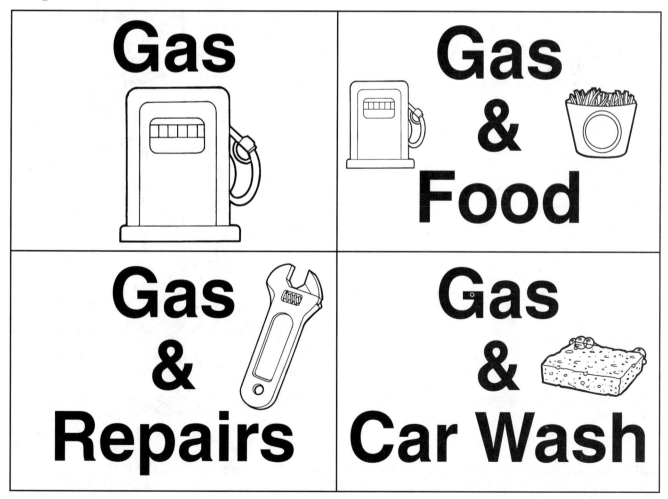

Gas Station *(cont.)*

Suggested Materials for the Gas Station

- boxes for pumps, cars, and cashier's window

- car advertisements

- car and truck brochures

- cash register

- clean gas can (new)

- pipe cleaners

- gallon milk containers (cleaned and empty)

- hub caps

- magazines about cars and trucks

- money (pages 246–247)

- overalls

- painter's caps

- plastic containers (recycled shampoo or dish soap bottles)

- rubber tubing or sections of an old garden hose

- silver paper plates

- aluminum foil

- tires (old ones from a tire supply store)

- tire gauges

- tire pumps

- tricycles, bikes, and assorted playground vehicles

- tool box

- tools to fix cars and bikes

- window wipers/scrapers

- vests

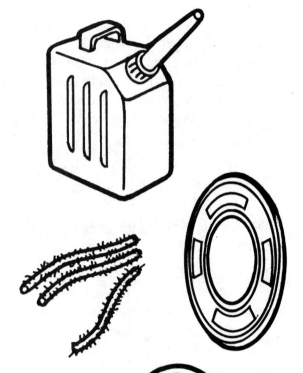

Optional: buckets, rags, sponges, towels, and a water source for a car wash

Gas Station (cont.)

Teacher Preparation

1. Make copies of the gas station markers on page 181 for the children to use to complete the introductory Gas Stations Graph described in the Lead Ins. The markers can be used to label the graph or multiple copies can be made so that each child can choose the appropriate marker to place on the graph.

2. Select an area outside for the Gas Station. There should be room for "cars" and other types of vehicles to pull up, get service, and drive on. There should be a separate area set aside for payment. This could include a walk-up window made from a large box with a hole cut out for the cashier to receive payments or a table with a cash register. This area can include other items for sale. Post lists of prices.

3. Consider setting aside an area to work on vehicles in need of repair. Use the labels on page 188 and on 253–255 in the Appendix. Add a toolbox with wrenches, screwdrivers, etc. Engage the children in discussions about car repairs. If old hub caps and other car parts are available, display them in the repair area.

4. After the children have painted the gas pump boxes, add sections of hose or rubber tubing to each. You may wish to have separate pumps for each type of fuel or combine the boxes to create multi-use pumps.

5. Use additional tubing to make a separate Air/Water station for cars and bikes to use. (See illustration.)

6. Set up an area for children to paint the boxes they will use to make cars. When the boxes dry, let them add headlights, gauges, wipers and other details. Headlights, tail lights, and windshield wipers to detail the cars can be found on pages 192–194. If possible, have the children cut these items out themselves. Add straps so that the "cars" can be worn. Use pipe cleaners for antennae and add a few for bumpers. Another option for bumpers might be to add strips of aluminum foil.

7. Determine prices for gas and other items that might be purchased in the station.

8. Decide if it will be feasible to have a car wash component for the Gas Station dramatic play center. Car washes work well in warm weather. School bikes, tricycles, and other vehicles can be lined up and washed with soapy water and then rinsed and dried. This activity is fun, good for fine and gross motor control, and guaranteed to get everyone wet! Be prepared and have extra towels and clothes.

9. Add stories about cars, trucks, and gas stations to the reading area.

10. Prepare money, credit cards, and checkbooks (pages 246–249).

11. The gas station could be another venue in which to serve snacks. Children can pull up, take care of their vehicles, and pick up quick, bagged snacks.

Gas Station *(cont.)*

Student Preparation

1. Vote on a name for the gas station and/or car wash. Make a sign for the gas station. Spell out the word G-A-S in large bubble letters and add pictures of different vehicles cut out from advertisements and magazines.

2. Make additional posters to advertise different items or services offered by the station. Cut out or draw pictures of motor oil, tires, fan belts, etc.

3. Review the labels and character names tags. Discuss costume options for the station. Painter's caps with the station name on them and vests should work. Overalls or coveralls might be a nice addition for the mechanics at the station to wear.

4. Paint tall, rectangular boxes to be used as gas pumps. Add the pump signs (page 187).

5. Decide on a price for a gallon of gas. Cut out the appropriate money and credit cards to be used in the center.

6. Decorate the cardboard-box cars to be used in the center.

7. Use index cards to make individual, personalized driver's licenses. Add school photos or draw pictures and sign them. Remember to carry a driver's license when operating a vehicle.

8. Make the appropriate money based on the established price lists for gas, services, and sundries.

9. Create an Open/Closed sign for the gas station or enlarge and decorate the one on page 245.

Vocabulary Building

attendant	full	pump
bald tire	funnel	regular
car wash	gas	service station
diesel	gauge	spare (tire)
donut (tire)	mechanic	supreme
empty	mini mart	tread
filling station	oil	unleaded
fuel	premium	wheel

Gas Station (cont.)

Literacy Development

- Create a class book of favorite cars. Encourage the children to draw or cut out pictures of their favorite cars and dictate or write stories about them. Why did they choose the vehicles? Where would they travel in the vehicles? Later, add the book to the reading center.

- Make two laminated sets of vehicle cards (pages 189–190). Use them in a literacy center to play matching games. Make more sets of the cards for patterning games.

- Enlarge the vehicle cards to color and make mini-books. Make book covers and decorate them with stickers, drawings, or magazine pictures. Add blank pages for favorite pictures to be included.

- Review color words. Make a graph of the color vehicle each child most often rides in/on. It can be the family car, a bus, a bike, or other vehicle or make a graph of the color of vehicle each child would most like to have someday.

- Use the concepts of "Full" and "Empty" to begin a discussion of opposites. See how many opposites can be listed.

- Go for a walk and compare wheeels on the cars parked along the way. Make a list of descriptive words when the walk is finished—*shiny*, *silver*, *pretty*, *cool*, etc. Design wheels on paper plates and display them in the classroom.

Numeracy Development

- Give cashiers ample opportunities to sell gas and to make change.

- Compare the number of tires on a unicycle, a bike, a tricycle, and a car. How many wheels does a school bus or a big delivery truck have? What kinds of vehicles have double wheels? What kinds of vehicles have no wheels? Make a "How Many Wheels?" chart and add to it as children think of more ideas.

- Measure out a gallon of water. Discuss how many gallons it takes to fill the tank of a car or a truck. Collect enough gallon containers (empty milk containers) to demonstrate how many gallons of gas a car or a truck might hold if the tank was full.

- Make a gas gauge using the pattern on page 191. Note the difference between having one gallon of gas and 10 gallons of gas. How many gallons on the gauge make a full tank, a half a tank, and an empty tank?

- Use the concepts of "Full" and "Empty" to discuss measurement. Set up a pouring table with standard and nonstandard measuring cups. Encourage children to demonstrate *empty*, *half full*, and *full*.

Gas Station *(cont.)*

Character Nametags

Attendant

Mechanic

Window Washer

Gas Station *(cont.)*

Pump Signs

Enlarge the signs to fit the boxes (pumps) to be used in the gas station.

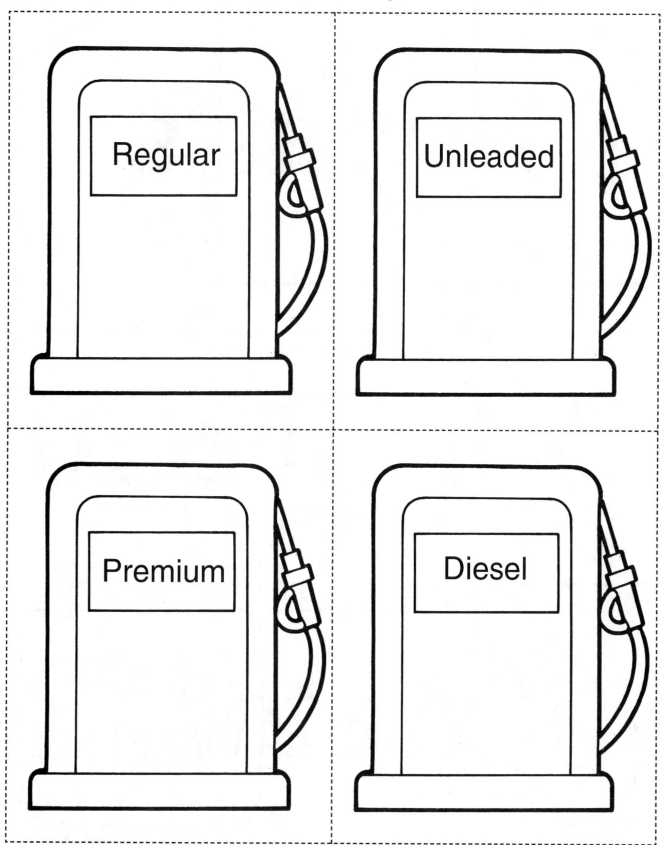

Signs

Repairs

Air

Food

Water

Gas Station *(cont.)*

Vehicle Cards

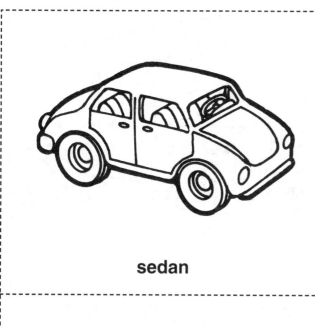

sedan

motorcycle

pickup

sports car

van

station wagon

Gas Station *(cont.)*

Vehicle Cards *(cont.)*

SUV

big rig

motor home

bus

camper

convertible

Gas Station (cont.)

Gas Gauge

Directions: Laminate the arrow and the gauge. Atttach the arrow to the gauge using a brad. Adjust the brad if necessary for easy movement.

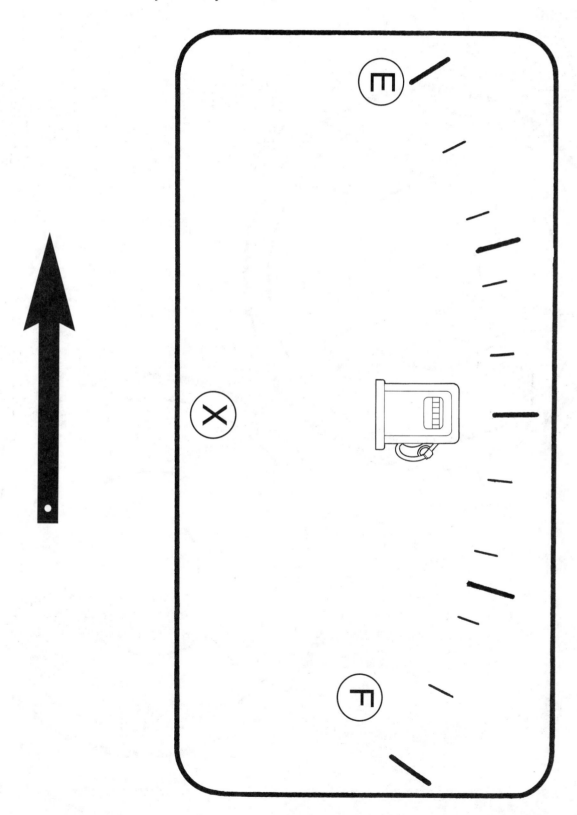

Gas Station *(cont.)*

Car Details

Determine if the car will have two headlights or four headlights. Cut out the appropriate number of headlights. Leave the lights white or color them yellow.

Headlights

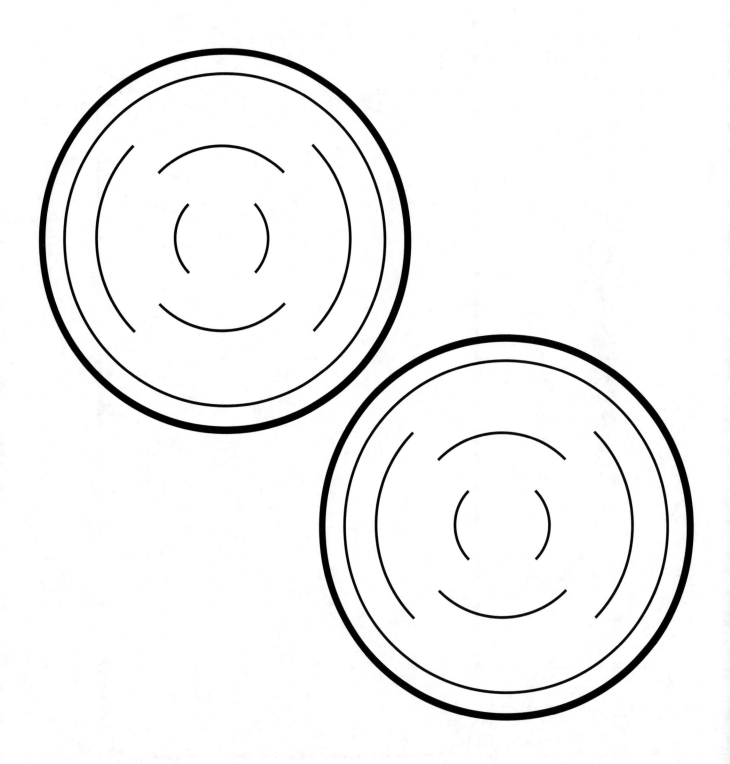

Gas Station *(cont.)*

Car Details *(cont.)*

Cut out the windshield wipers and the taillights. Color the taillights red.

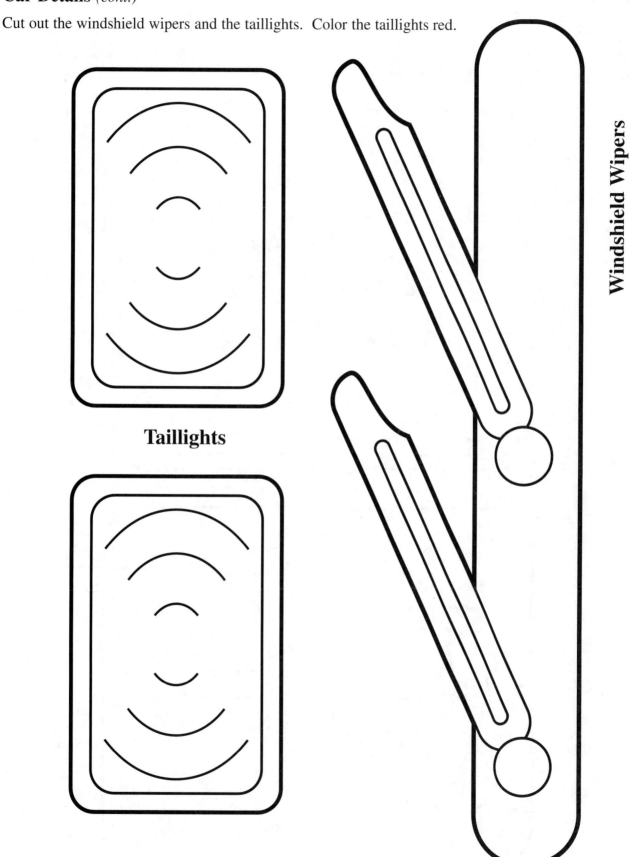

Taillights

Windshield Wipers

Gas Station *(cont.)*

Car Details *(cont.)*

Gas Cap

Cut out the two sections of the gas cap. Color the letters G-A-S. Staple the two sections together on the left side. The gas cap picture should be on top.

Going Camping

Lead Ins

- Bring a sleeping bag and a camping lantern or a flashlight to the class meeting area. Ask children to identify the items and to discuss when they might be used. Guide the children toward the idea of camping. Ask who has been camping before. If no children have been camping, describe a camping trip to them. If there are children who have been camping, ask them to share their experiences. Has anyone camped out in his or her backyard?

- Share some dehydrated camping food with the children. Freeze-dried ice cream is always a big surprise! Give each child a small piece, explain that it is something sweet and see who can guess what it is. Discuss why it is prepared and packaged as it is. Explain that often, campers hike long distances before they set up their campsites and they need to make their packs as light as possible.

- Build a "campfire" with children using 3 or 4 logs (if you must, substitute cardboard tubes from paper towel rolls for logs), kindling (again, if necessary, toilet paper rolls will work) and some red and yellow cellophane paper. Begin with some kindling. Explain that it is best to start small and build up a fire. Pretend to light the kindling and add a bit of cellophane amongst the twigs. While you wait for the fire to "build" talk about fire safety. Remind children that they should never play with matches or try to light a fire. After a while, add larger sticks and more cellophane flames to the fire. Continue adding more wood and flames. (See illustrations.) Take this opportunity to reinforce fire safety rules.

- Make a list of things that you should not do when camping. Include littering, straying from the group, and disturbing animals and their habitats.

- Introduce books about camping and stargazing. Discuss activities that people do while camping—fishing, canoeing, stargazing, hiking, swimming, sleeping outdoors, etc. Make a chart or graph of the thing each child would most like to do when camping. Use the picture cards on pages 201–202 to note choices on the graph or chart. (**Note:** The cards can be reduced for this activity, if appropriate.)

Going Camping *(cont.)*

Suggested Materials for Going Camping

- air mattresses
- backpacks
- light blue bulletin-board paper
- camping supplies magazines
- canteens or individual, labeled water bottles
- children's books about nature and camping
- cooler
- field guides about trees, birds, and animals
- flashlights
- grill or oven rack
- lawn chairs
- logs
- picnic baskets
- picnic blankets
- picnic table
- pots, pans, dishes, and utensils
- red and yellow cellophane
- rocks or concrete blocks (for the fire pit)
- scale
- sleeping bags
- small brooms
- tents
- trail guides and hiking manuals

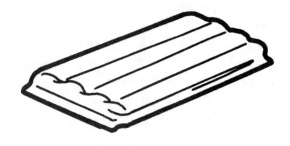

Camping Food

- condiments (ketchup, relish, mustard, etc)
- dehydrated food packets
- dehydrated ice cream
- hamburgers and buns
- hotdogs and buns
- ingredients for trail mix
- ingredients for s'mores (chocolate bars, graham crackers, marshmallow crème)

Going Camping *(cont.)*

Teacher Preparation

1. Show the children the parts of the tent before it is set up. Ask them to guess what shape it will be when it is put together. Have them estimate how big/tall it will be when it is set up. If appropriate, have them help set it up. Determine ahead of time if children will be allowed to wear shoes and/or eat inside the tent. Have a small broom handy for brushing out the tent each day. (Note: If a tent is not available, use a series of large appliance boxes or large blankets strung over ropes, or a canopy, to create a tent-like structure.)

2. Set up a campsite. Arrange the campsite to include an area for the tent, a table for food, dishes, and the cooler, and whatever other materials are available. If possible, arrange a ring of rocks to surround the "campfire" (see Lead In). Place a grill over the rocks when the fire is ready and it is time to cook. Supply pots and pans for cooking.

3. Determine a maximum number of campers in the tent at a given time and post a number card outside the tent to remind the children. Number cards are located in the Appendix on pages 242–244.

4. Label the different areas in the campsite. Create a chart to make sure that everyone has had a chance to tend the fire, sweep out the tent, wash the dishes, etc.

5. Set up the campfire described in the Lead In. Review safety precautions and remind students that this fire is make believe and that they should never try to start a real fire. Explain that, each day in the camping center, a different child will be the Fire Tender. That child will be in charge of making the fire and later putting the fire out.

6. Decorate the classroom with posters and pictures of campsites, trees, star constellations, and woodland scenes.

7. Add stories to the reading area about hiking, camping, walking in the woods, stargazing, etc.

8. Make s'mores or trail mix (page 203) for a special snack.

9. Plan a special camping event. Have a barbecue. Cook and serve hot dogs and hamburgers outside on picnic blankets. Turn it into an evening event and invite children's families. After the meal, sing songs around the "campfire."

10. If the children nap at school, have them bring sleeping bags for a special treat. Set up the "campfire" in the middle of the sleeping bags and tell special stories before children begin their rest period. For an added treat, put glow-in-the-dark stars on the ceiling in the nap area and turn off the lights.

11. Make two or more sets of the Things to Do Camping cards (pages 201–202). Place them in the classroom so the children can play concentration or matching games.

Going Camping *(cont.)*

Student Preparation

1. Vote on a name for the campsite. Consider naming it after a local park or a familiar landmark. Make a sign and decorate it with pictures cut from camping supplies magazines.

2. Review the labels and character names tags. Discuss costume options. Try hats, bandanas, sunglasses, and backpacks.

3. Create a mural on light blue bulletin-board paper. First, paint the ground on the paper. Add some glue to brown tempera paint ($\frac{1}{2}$ paint and $\frac{1}{2}$ glue) and sprinkle some potting soil, pine cones, pine needles, seed pods, or leaves on the "ground" before it dries. When the ground dries, paint a sun, trees, flowers, rocks, and paths. Cut out pictures of forest animals and birds and add them to the mural.

4. Decorate a paper tablecloth or weave paper place mats for a special camp meal.

5. Decide on a menu for the end of the center picnic. Brainstorm camping foods and then vote on the favorites.

Vocabulary Building

backpack	constellations	kindling	stargazing
camper	gear	lantern	stuff bag
campsite	grill	roast	trail
clearing	hiking	s'mores	

Going Camping *(cont.)*

Literacy Development

- Compare different aspects of camping to being at home. Start by comparing sleeping in a sleeping bag to sleeping in a bed. Which is more comfortable and why? Is it more fun to sleep in—a sleeping bag or in a bed? Is it easier to cook on a campfire or to cook on a stove or in an oven? What other things are different when camping—washing dishes, bathing, entertainment, etc.

- Create a class book about camping. Use photographs from family trips or pictures from magazines to prompt stories or to create pages children can label. See how many different items the children can name and label in a campsite. Later, add the book to the reading center.

- Share stories with children about life long ago. Imagine what it would be like to live without electricity or modern transportation. How would you get to school? How would you listen to music? What would you do to entertain yourself without the television or video games?

- Use the Things to Do Camping cards on pages 201–202. Arrange the cards in order of preference. Show what activity you like to do the most and the least and explain why.

- After eating s'mores, guess why the chocolate, marshmallow, and graham cracker treat is called s'mores. Could it be that you always want "some more"?

Numeracy Development

- Discuss the tent. What shape(s) is it? How many zippers does the tent have? How many sides does it have? How many poles were used to set it up? How many stakes does it have?

- Count and sort the different ingredients in the Trail Mix. Create a graph using one piece of each ingredient. Allow each child to place a piece of his favorite ingredient in the appropriate square.

- Weigh and measure a collection of flashlights. Find the heaviest, the lightest, the smallest, and the longest.

- Practice rolling up a sleeping bag. How many rolls does it take? If the sleeping bag belongs in a stuff bag, how many "stuffs" does it take to get the whole thing in the bag?

- Measure out the ingredients for the s'mores or the trail mix and make a treat for snack time. Use the recipes on page 203.

- Discuss distances. Compare how long it might take to walk/hike somewhere versus driving in a car. Perhaps a teacher or parent could be asked to drive a distance and later children could walk the same distance and compare times.

- Go on a nature walk and count trees, animals, insects, or other items.

Going Camping *(cont.)*

Character Nametags

Backpacker

Hiker

Fire Tender

Going Camping *(cont.)*

Things to Do Camping

fish

canoe

stargaze

hike

Going Camping *(cont.)*

Things to Do Camping *(cont.)*

sleep outdoors

roast marshmallows

picnic

cook at a campfire

Going Camping *(cont.)*

Recipes

S'mores

Ingredients per student
- graham crackers (two squares)
- marshmallow creme
- plastic knives
- section of a chocolate bar, approximately 2" (5 cm) square

Optional Materials
- heat source to roast marshmallows
- marshmallows
- long skewer or wire hanger

Directions (no heat source)
1. Supply each child with two graham cracker squares, one square of hocolate, and some marshmallow creme.
2. Lay the two crackers side by side. Place the chocolate on one cracker square.
3. Spread marshmallow creme on the cracker that does not have chocolate on it.
4. Press the two crackers together.

Alternative: If a heat source is available, prepare the hanger or skewer and place a marshmallow on the end. Help each child hold the marshmallow over the heat source until it is lightly browned. Lay the roasted marshmallow on the chocolate and cover it with the other cracker. Pull out the hanger or skewer and let the concoction cool.

Allergy Alert: Be sure the ingredients used are appropriate for the children who will be participating in the activity.

Trail Mix

Choose from the following list of ingredients to make your special camper mix.
- coconut
- dried fruit
- raisins
- chocolate chips
- cereal
- sunflower seeds
- nuts
- small, fish-shaped crackers

Directions
1. Mix each of the ingredients chosen from the list above together in a large bowl.
2. Scoop out $\frac{1}{2}$ cup of the mixture and place it in a flat-bottomed coffee filter or small bag for each child.

Allergy Alert: Be sure the ingredients used are appropriate for the children who will be participating in the activity.

Nature Explorers

Lead Ins

- Bring in a collection of items found in nature and share them with the class. Bring rocks, a plant, a cup of soil, some crickets or other bugs in a jar, flowers from the garden, and some leaves from a tree nearby. Try to bring a combination of living and nonliving things. Discuss each item and its relationship to nature.

- Share a collection of items from nature and man-made objects from the classroom. Create a chart for the items in each category.

- Brainstorm a list of nature items to explore in the surrounding area. Add to the list as interest grows. Capitalize on the surrounding area. Are there earthworms or snails out after a rain shower or new leaves sprouting on a tree? Perhaps birds are building a new nest nearby.

- Introduce books about nature. Find out more about each item explored.

- Share stories as well as science-based texts and field guides pertinent to the area. Look to the different books for ideas and possible projects.

- Establish a weather calendar in the classroom. Design weather symbols for each type of weather expected. Each day, note the type of weather on the calendar.

- Gather tadpoles from a nearby pond or stream. Sometimes large puddles near a walking path are a good source. Keep them in a fishbowl to start. Add water and foliage from the source. **Note:** Once the tadpoles have become frogs, return them to their original habitat.

- Sit outside and listen for sounds of nature. Can you hear birds, crickets, running water, squirrels, or trees blowing in the breeze? Make a list of all the things heard by the children. On another day, list all the things in nature that can be smelled while sitting outside. Continue making lists each day for all the senses. Compare the lists.

Nature Explorers *(cont.)*

Suggested Materials for Nature Explorers

- backpacks
- barometer
- birds nests
- books about bugs, insects, trees, birds, and small mammals
- bug nets
- bulletin-board paper
- children's books with nature themes
- color paint chips
- fish bowl
- fish tank (to hold dirt, not water—small leaks won't matter)
- insect nests and spider egg sacs
- jars
- magnifying glasses
- milk cartons
- netting
- posters related to nature
- pots and other planting containers
- rubber bands
- rulers
- scales
- seedlings
- seeds
- small terrariums
- soil
- thermometer (weather)
- toilet paper rolls (2 per child)
- watering cans
- wheat berry grass seeds (purchase them in a health food store)

NATURE

Nature Explorers *(cont.)*

Teacher Preparation

This outdoor dramatic play center works well in spring or early summer depending on your location. Plan on extended explorations of the school grounds, the backyard, or the neighborhood. Look around and ascertain the facets of nature that will be the most interesting and available to study. The key to this center is to draw from your immediate surroundings. Could you start a garden? Do weather conditions change enough to warrant investigation? Can you raise tadpoles in the classroom or track their growth in a local pond? What kinds of animals are available to observe?

1. Gather attire for the naturalists to wear while exploring, such as bandanas, baseball caps, and homemade binoculars. Another option would be to make different headbands for different nature explorers. Antennae could be added for entomologists, leaves and flowers could decorate the botanists/gardeners headbands, and wings on the bird watchers bands. Yet another option would be headbands that the children could decorate with different naturalist symbols (page 214).

2. Start seed and leaf collections in the classroom. Use egg cartons, shoe boxes, and other small containers to house the collections. Incorporate child-made signs to the collection area and add reference books pertaining to each topic.

3. Add books to the reading area that relate to the different areas of nature being observed. Share these books during group gatherings. Extend the books with art and science projects.

4. Decide on the character nametags that will be appropriate for the group. Will they all be naturalists or will the titles be more specific and include botanists, meteorologists, and entomologists? Use pages 212–213.

5. Display posters (in the classroom or outside) depicting different facets of nature—weather, plant lifecycles, trees and flowers, insects, etc.

6. Invite visitors to talk about different facets of nature. Find out if there is a local wildlife sanctuary, animal lending library, or animal care center in the area that deals with wild animals. Invite someone from a local nursery to come into the classroom.

7. Determine what will work at your site and begin setting up the different observation areas. Some start-up suggestions are offered on the following page.

Nature Explorers (cont.)

Teacher Preparation (cont.)

Plants and Trees

- Tend an existing garden or start a class garden. Plot out an area of land to plant seedlings. The plants can be started indoors earlier on windowsills or in terrariums.

- In more urban settings it may work to start a garden using pots and tubs. You can sprout sweet potatoes or avocado seeds indoors in a sunny spot.

- Ascertain which plants and trees are common to the area. Are the trees broad-leaved or are they evergreens? Are the trees sprouting new leaves, flowers, or fruits? Pick out a tree or two. Look for trees with distinctive bark, interesting leaves, flowers, or seed pods. Periodically, observe these trees and note changes.

- Observe pollen on different flowers. Watch, from a safe distance, as different insects fly from flower to flower. Explain that the insects are carrying pollen stuck on their legs from one flower to another, which pollinates them.

Birds, Rodents, and Small Animals

- Coax hummingbirds or other local birds to the area with outdoor feeders. (It is best to set up the feeders well in advance of the center to guarantee visitors.) Are there visible nests in nearby trees? Can you spot birds carrying food or nesting materials back to their nests?

- Make nests using sticks, mud, twigs, grasses, pine needles, and other items found in the area.

- Start a collection of birds' nests. Note the different items used to make them. Sometimes, bits of string, tissue, and other items dropped on the ground can be found incorporated in the nests. Look at books about birds and their nests. Learn more about different bird habitats.

- Squirrels and chipmunks are great to observe in trees. If there are nuts, acorns, or seed pods in the area, collect them to use for counting activities indoors. If it rains, try to spot a squirrel using its tail for an umbrella to stay dry.

- Find a lizard to watch while it suns itself. Explain that lizards are cold-blooded animals and need a heat source to maintain their body temperature.

- Take care of different school animals or pets. Learn about their natural habitats, diets, sleeping habits, etc.

Nature Explorers (cont.)

Teacher Preparation *(cont.)*

Insects and Bugs

- Create a bug habitat. Set a terrarium up outside. Use an old fish tank or clear plastic container. Fill the terrarium(s) about halfway with potting soil. Add a combination of grass seeds, bird seed, wheat berry seeds, or small plants. Place a branch and a rock or two on top of the soil in the terrarium. Some insects and bugs need cover and/or moisture. Encourage children to add worms, caterpillars, isopods (pill bugs and sow bugs), snails, spiders, and other creatures as they find them. Keep a tally sheet nearby to record creatures as they are added.

- Look into purchasing lady bird beetles (ladybugs) or crickets. Ladybugs can be purchased at nurseries and can be added to vegetable gardens suffering from aphids. Crickets can be kept in the classroom. Male crickets chirp by rubbing their back legs together.

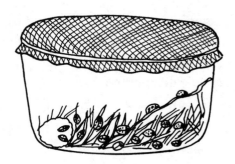

- Ants and bees are both interesting insects to study since they live and work in colonies run by females. Learn about their societies and act out the different roles in each:

    Bees—queen, drones, workers

    Ants—queen, scouts, room builders, food gatherers, nurses

    Silkworms and butterfly gardens can be ordered through Carolina Biological Supplies (http: //www.carolina.com).

Teacher Note: Silkworms eat only mulberry leaves. If you do not have access to a mulberry tree, don't try silkworms!

Nature Explorers (cont.)

Student Preparation

1. Divide up into groups to create signs for each of the collections that will be displayed in the classroom. Use drawings, pictures from magazines, and nature items to embellish the signs.

2. Create binoculars by taping two toilet paper rolls together. Punch holes in the outside of the each tube. Attach string or yarn so that the binoculars can be worn around the neck.

3. Make bug collectors out of milk cartons. Clean out the container and cut "windows" in one or two of the sides. Tape netting over the windows. Jars make great containers as well. Holes can be poked in the lids or the lids can be discarded and netting can be stretched over the top and held in place with rubber bands. Glass jars should be handled with care at all times. Bug collectors made of paper or cardboard can be carried around during nature walks but the glass containers should remain inside, on tables or shelves for observing bugs.

4. Review rules for safety and respectfully observing living plants, insects, and animals. Discuss the importance of observing without disturbing animals and their habitats. With a teacher, make a list of important rules and post it in the classroom.

Vocabulary Building

abdomen	cocoon	meteorologist
antennae	collector	nectar
arachnid	container	needles
birder	entomologist	ornithologist
botanist	evergreen	pollen
broad-leaved	head	soil
bug	insect	terrarium
chrysalis	larvae	thorax

Nature Explorers *(cont.)*

Literacy Development

- Create a class book entitled "The Colors in Nature." Use large sheets of construction paper in the colors of the rainbow. It is best to put two or three sheets of each color in the book. Label each page to enhance color word recognition. Staple the pages together and decorate the cover. Keep the book in the writing/crafts area. Take turns looking through magazines for pictures of things found in nature. Cut the pictures out and glue them to a page. Periodically share the book during group time to see what new pictures have been found. See who can find those items. Later, add the book to the reading center.

- Paint a large rainbow to display outside. Follow the color order of a traditional rainbow—*red, orange, yellow, green, blue, indigo* and *violet*. Label each color of the rainbow using the labels on pages 215–216. Review the color word labels once or twice a week.

- Talk about leaves. A leaf's job is to make food for a tree. Sort the leaf collection by color, shape, or type. Are the leaves broad-leaved and do they all fall off the tree in winter (deciduous)? Are the leaves more needle-like and do they seem to stay on the tree all year round (evergreen)?

- Use paint chips or crayons to go on a color hunt. Give children different colored chips or crayons and have them find that color in nature. If there is a limited variety of color, give one color at a time. See how many variations the children can locate.

- Place snails on a large sheet of black paper. Have the children observe them as the glide along the paper. While watching, have them dictate descriptions of the snails and their movements. What do their antennae do? Notice the trail that the snail leaves as it meanders along the paper. It will be shiny. Watch them eat lettuce leaves.

- Keep individual observation diaries of discoveries, experiments, and observations. Use the mini-book provided on pages 217–219 to get started. Draw pictures of the different plants, birds, and insects that are observed. Dictate or write stories to accompany the drawings. Add blank pages as needed.

- Chronicle life sequences of flowers, butterflies, frogs, birds, etc. Note the changes at each stage. Use the charts and mini-books on pages 220–222 as prompts.

- Play charades. Divide up into small groups and act out different animal and insect behaviors. Be a squirrel gathering nuts, an ant carrying a huge piece of food back to the ant hill, or a bird flying home with a new piece of nesting material for the nest.

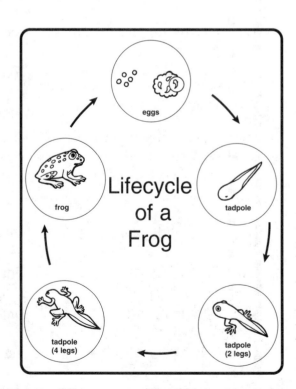

Nature Explorers *(cont.)*

Numeracy Development

- Keep a weather calendar for the duration of the center. Note the weather each day—sunny, windy, rainy, warm, cool, etc. At the end of the center, count and tally each type of day and transfer the information to a chart or graph.

- Count seeds, pinecones, acorns, etc. Sort them into groups of specified numbers or by size or shape.

- Talk about true insects. Learn the names of the three body parts—head, thorax, and abdomen. Note that insects have two antennae, six legs, and three body parts. Legs, and wings when present, are part of the thorax. Draw insects.

- Compare spiders (arachnids) to insects. Spiders have two body parts and eight legs.

- Have insect races and time the insects to see how long it takes them to reach a certain location. One way to do this is to draw a large 16" (40 cm) circle on a sheet of light colored bulletin-board paper. Gather a few pill bugs or sow bugs (isopods) and place them under a cup in the center of the children. On an agreed upon signal, set a timer, lift the cup and see how long it takes one of the bugs to cross the finish line.

- Make caterpillars using egg cartons and pipe cleaners. Count the sections. How many sections long is the caterpillar? How many legs does it have? Add four tissue-paper wings and "fly" them around the room.

- Measure the growth of different plants in the garden. (For indoor gardens, plant wheat berry seeds. They grow in a week.) Make craft stick rulers to measure the growth.

- Keep track of the temperature on a chart. Does it vary from day to day; from morning to noon to evening?

- Melt ice cubes and time the melting process. Do cubes melt faster early in the morning, at noon, or in the late afternoon?

- Count legs on the different bugs, spiders, and insects studied. Insects always have six legs, spiders have eight legs, and bugs can have different numbers of legs. How many pairs of legs do each have? What about centipedes and millipedes?

Nature Explorers (cont.)

Character Nametags

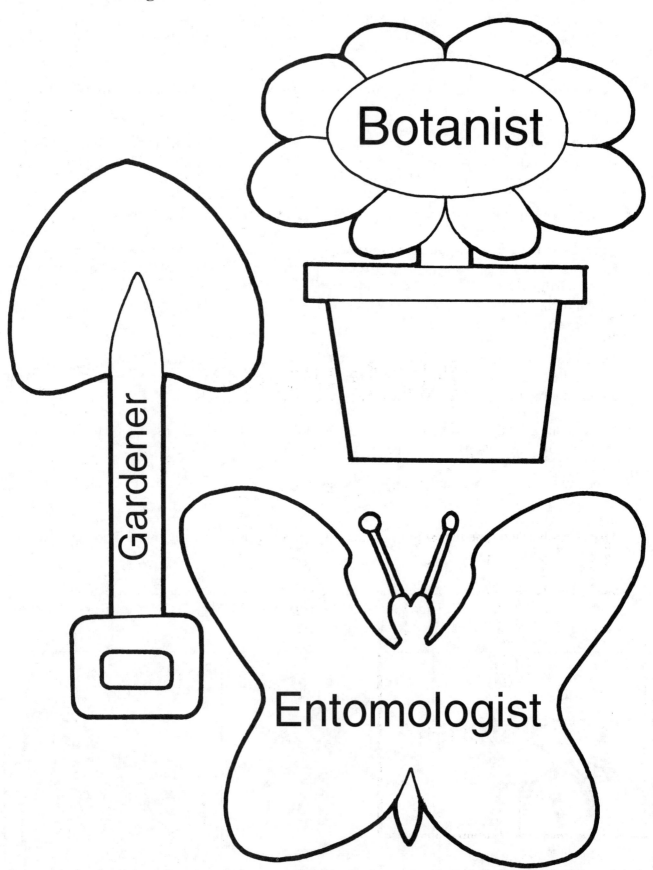

Nature Explorers *(cont.)*

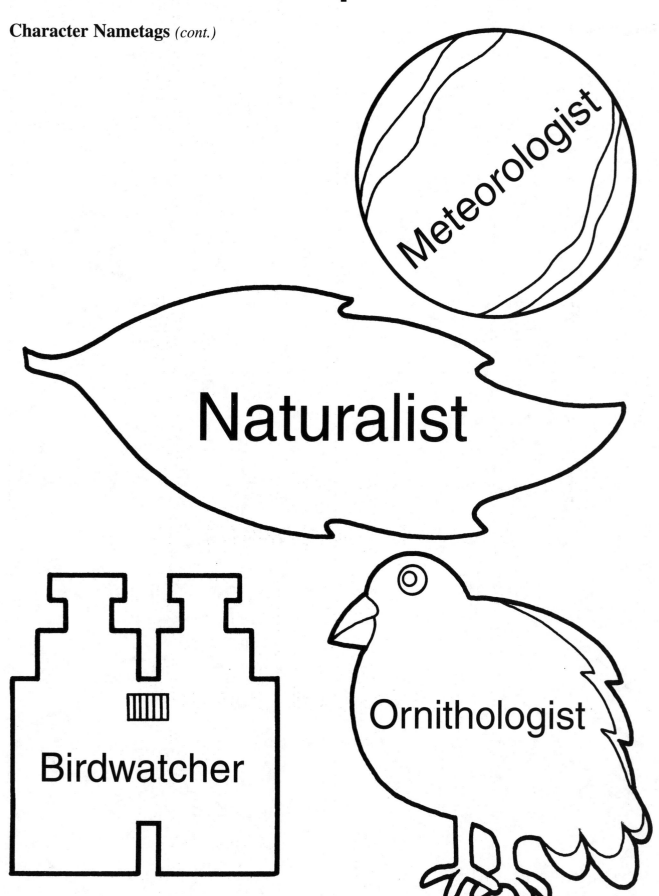

Meteorologist

Naturalist

Birdwatcher

Ornithologist

Nature Explorers *(cont.)*

Naturalist Symbols

Leaves

Birds

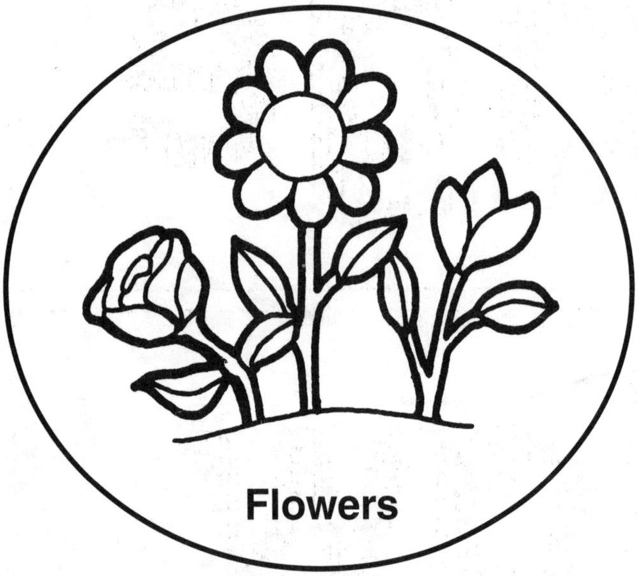

Flowers

Small Animals

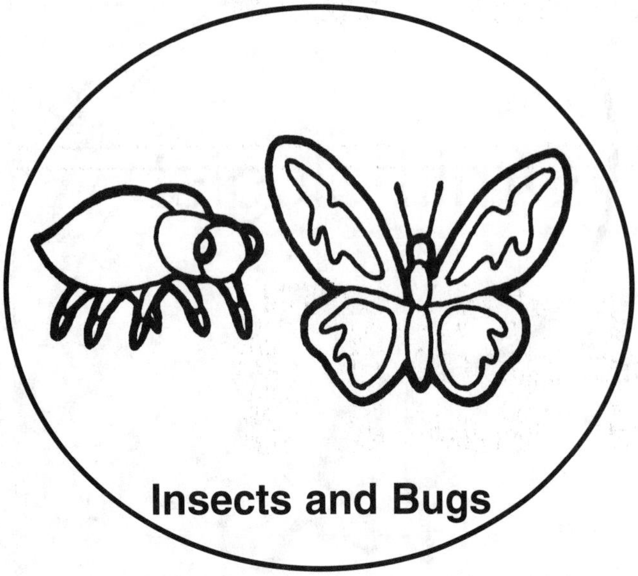

Insects and Bugs

Weather

Rainbow Colors

Red

Orange

Yellow

Green

Rainbow Colors *(cont.)*

Blue

Indigo

Violet

RAINBOW

Nature Explorers <small>(cont.)</small>

Observation Log

Weather

Insects and Bugs

Nature Explorers *(cont.)*

Trees

Plants and Flowers

Nature Explorers *(cont.)*

Observation Log *(cont.)*

Animals

Birds

Nature Explorers (cont.)

The Life Cycle of a Flower (Sequencing Cards)

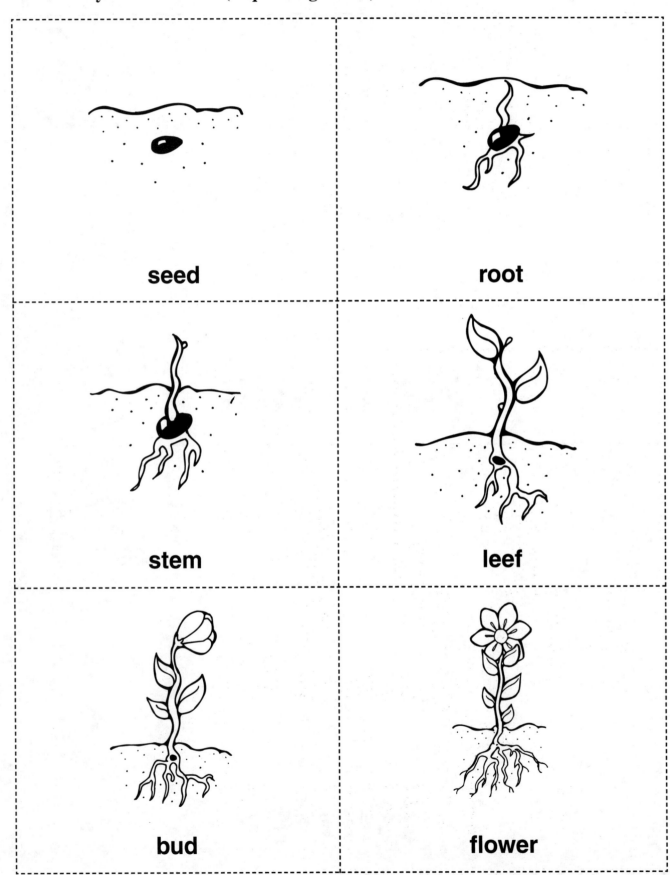

seed

root

stem

leef

bud

flower

Nature Explorers *(cont.)*

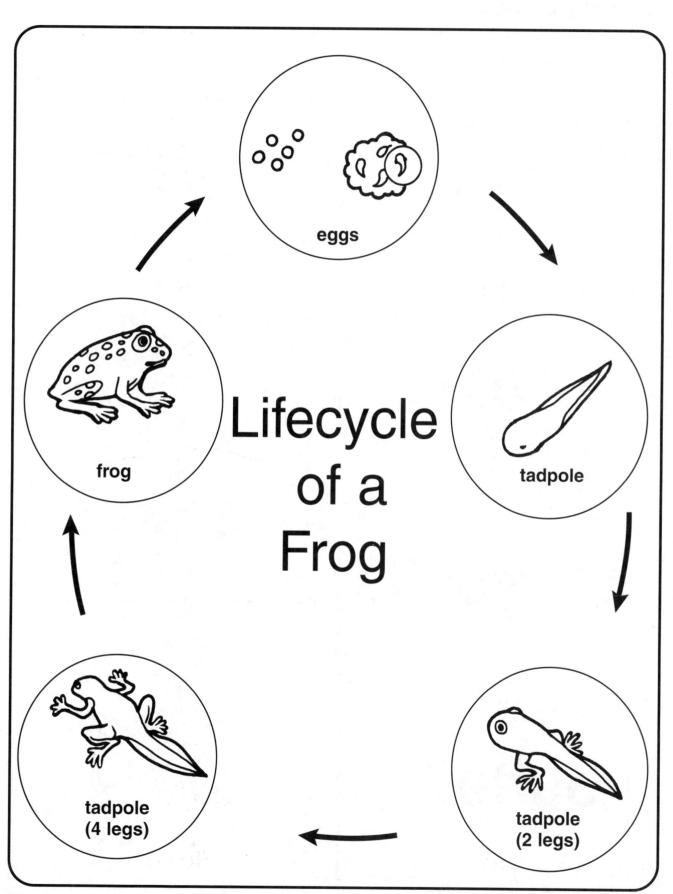

Nature Explorers *(cont.)*

The Lifecycle of a Butterfly

Cut out the two strips. Staple the word strip section on top of the picture strip section. Cut the top page on the dashed lines to create a flip book. Color the second page.

egg	
larva	
chrysalis	
butterfly	

Panning for Gold

Lead Ins

- Bring some gold jewelry and decorative objects to group time. Ask what the items are made of and where gold is found.

- Explain that gold is found in the ground and in streams. It is mined in a variety of ways. People can pan for it in streams and rivers or dig for it in the ground or in mountainsides.

- Discuss the Gold Rush (California, 1848). Explain that people traveled West when they heard that gold had been discovered. Discuss the different tools and methods that were used to extract gold from the land, streams, and rivers. Some miners used shovels to dig in the ground and into the sides of mountains. Other miners panned for gold in the streams using small round pans. Still other miners working by streams and rivers created sluice boxes that worked like large strainers to search for gold. All the miners worked hard to find gold because it was, and still is, very valuable. They wanted to become rich.

- Show children a mining pan (pie pan). Explain that they will be using the pans to pan for gold, just like the gold miners of old! Go outside to the claim site and demonstrate how the pan works (see Teacher Preparation, step 2).

- Brainstorm a list of participants at a mining site. Mention miners, those who used pans to work the streams, and sluice box operators (Teacher Preparation, step 5). Add the people who ran the bank, the store, and perhaps those who served food.

- Introduce books about rocks, minerals, and the Gold Rush. Use this dramatic play center as an introduction to starting an ongoing classroom rock collection.

Panning for Gold *(cont.)*

Suggested Materials for Panning for Gold

- backpacks

- balance scales

- bandanas

- books about rocks and minerals

- broad-brimmed hats

- canteens

- children's books about gold rushes and mining

- claim certificates (page 231)

- gold spray paint

- gravel

- magazines and advertisements with pictures of items made of gold

- pie tins (aluminum or a heavier metal)

- plastic tape to mark off the mining area

- pyrite samples

- rock collections

- rulers or measuring sticks

- scales

- small shovels

- stakes or plastic garden poles (approximately three feet tall)

- wagons

- water source

- water tables or large tubs

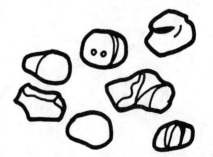

Panning for Gold *(cont.)*

Teacher Preparation

1. Establish an area to pan for gold. This can be the sand area at the school or a series of tubs or water tables filled with sand. Long water tables work best to simulate streams of water or sluice boxes. Post the sign made by the students and appropriate labels. (See illustration below.)

2. Gather pie pans to pan for gold. Teach children to pan for gold using a swirling motion. Enlarge the pictures on page 230 to aid in the demonstration. For younger children, create strainer-type pans. Use a hammer and a nail to poke holes in the pie pans. To be safe, flip the pans upside down to poke the holes. Then, turn the pans right side up and hammer down the rough edges of each hole.

3. Make "gold" nuggets. Wash gravel, dry it, and spread it out on layers of newspaper. Use gold spray paint to paint the gravel and let it dry. Then, turn the gravel over to spray paint the other side. Let the "gold" dry. For added interest, spray paint a few larger pebbles and rocks. When the children are not there, spread the nuggets over the area. Arrange some nuggets to form a vein, others in clumps and still others in a scattered pattern. Cover all but a few "nuggets" of gold with dirt or sand. Keep some gold hidden where the children can not find it. Have it ready to restock the claim area as needed depending on how long the site will be in use. Keep an eye on students to make sure everyone is finding some "gold." **Note:** Bury the larger pieces a little deeper or keep them for later when interest is beginning to wane to renew interest.

4. Stake out the class claim area on the first day the dramatic play center is open for exploration. Place stakes in the four corners of the area and run plastic tape around it. Explain that the area will be available at certain times and that they cannot dig for gold in areas other than the mining site. Suggest that the other areas are claims that belong to other people.

5. If students will have access to water and a hose, set up a sluice box using the water table. Allow students to fill buckets with earth or sand from the claim site. Have them take turns dumping their buckets in the water table and running water over it to search for gold. Use strainers and sifters as well as pans. Encourage them to yell "Eureka!" from the Latin "I have found," when they "strike gold."

Panning for Gold (cont.)

Teacher Preparation (cont.)

6. Set up an area to weigh and measure the gold that is discovered each day. Keep a tally sheet nearby to log in each student's find.

7. Decorate the classroom with pictures of gold coins, nuggets, and products made of gold.

8. Establish costumes for the miners, such as bandanas and broad-brimmed hats. Fill backpacks with small shovels and pans. Add canteens, if possible.

9. Determine a maximum number of participants at the mining site and place an enlarged number card nearby to remind the children. Number cards can be found in the Appendix on pages 242–244.

10. Decorate a wagon to look like an old buckboard or covered wagon. Use the wagon to carry the mining tools, gold when it is found, and lunches or snacks to and from the claim site.

11. Add stories about mining and books about rocks and minerals to the reading area.

12. Arrange for a special guest—a rock collector, someone in the jewelry or mining industry, or perhaps an historian.

Panning for Gold *(cont.)*

Student Preparation

1. Crumple up a large piece of brown wrapping paper and smooth it out to make a sign. Name the site after the school, the town, or the street on which the school is located.

2. Review the labels and character names tags. Look in books about the time of the Gold Rush and discuss costume options. Discuss what life might have been like without modern conveniences.

3. Create bags to store each miner's gold as it is found. Decorate brown paper lunch bags or small felt bags.

4. Gather mining pans. Create an area to store the different tools that will be used. Make labels and count the pans, shovels, etc.

5. Make a collage of items made of gold. Cut out pictures of gold coins, jewelry, decorative items, picture frames, etc. Use gold crayons to add drawings to the collage. Embellish the collage using gold crayons and gold glitter.

6. Start a class rock collection with a sample of pyrite (fool's gold). Supply reference books with color pictures to help students find out more about the rocks in the collection.

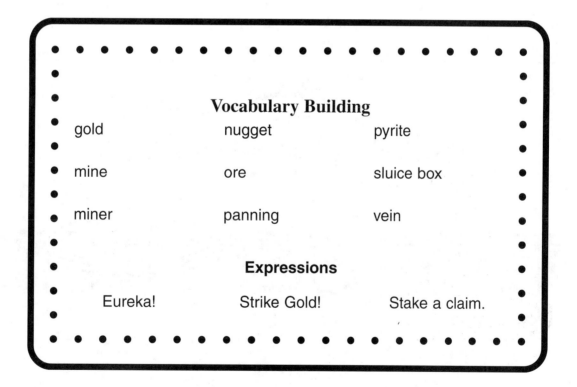

Vocabulary Building

gold	nugget	pyrite
mine	ore	sluice box
miner	panning	vein

Expressions

Eureka!   Strike Gold!   Stake a claim.

Panning for Gold *(cont.)*

Literacy Development

- Create a class newspaper or book about striking gold. Add pictures taken at the dig site or during weighing and measuring sessions. Have children summarize stories they have heard in class about the Gold Rush. Add children's descriptions of their own experiences finding gold. Later, make copies of the newspaper to send home or add the book to the reading center. Let children take turns taking the book home to share with their families.
- Explore the meaning of the expressions, "Eureka!" and "struck gold!"
- Discuss what it means to "stake a claim." Is it the same as having a turn in a center?
- Discuss different uses for gold—jewelry, art objects, electronics, dentistry, money, decorations, etc. Make a list and add to it during the lifetime of the center.

Numeracy Development

- Count nuggets of gold. Count the nuggets by twos. Sort them into piles of five, ten, or more as numeracy skills improve.
- Have each child weigh each day's find. Keep charts to indicate the amounts found. Later, weigh the total amount of gold mined at the site.
- Measure how deep the holes are that are dug each day by the miners.
- Establish a bank indoors to store the gold. Make a safe, using an old box. Choose a new banker each day. Encourage the children to keep passbooks to log their finds. (Enlarge the sample below.) This will give them practice measuring and writing numbers. It will also reinforce learning to recognize the days of the week.

Passbook

Miner's Name _____

Account Number

Day	Amount
Monday	
Tuesday	
Wednesday	
Thursday	
Friday	

Panning for Gold *(cont.)*

Character Nametags

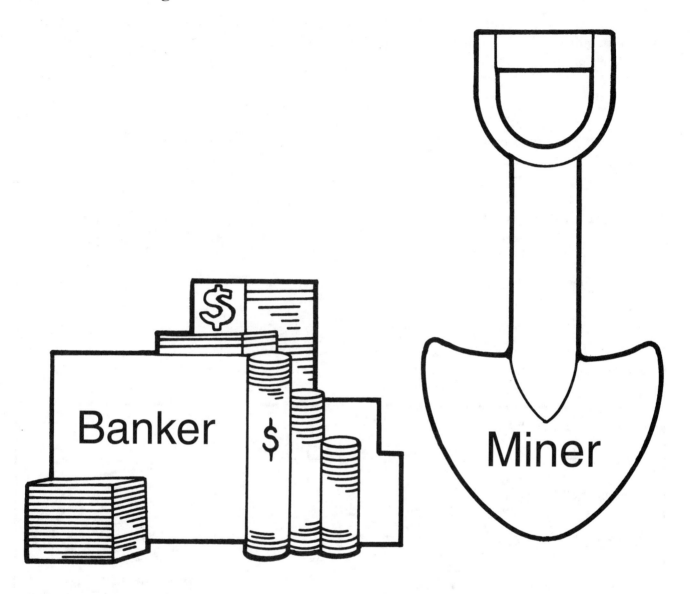

Banker

Miner

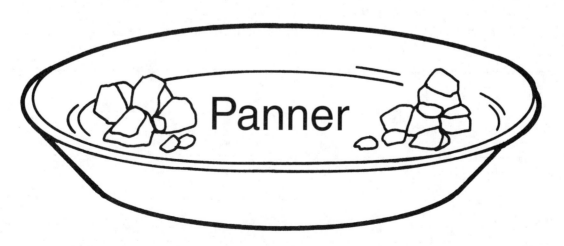

Panner

Panning for Gold *(cont.)*

How to Pan

Panning for gold is a bit trickier than it looks. For very young children, use the pans that have holes punched into them. For older children, or those with more advanced motor skills, try panning with regular pie pans as shown below.

1. Have each student take a small scoop of sand from the bucket and put it in a pie tin.

2. Place about $^1\!/_2$ cup (120 mL) of water in the tin.

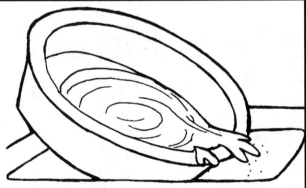

3. Over a sink or second bucket, have the student swirl the tin around in an orbital motion until the sand and water are washed out.

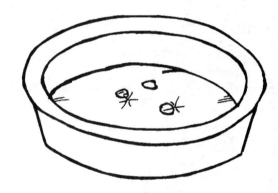

4. The heavier gold gravel should remain.

CLAIM CERTIFICATE

MINING CLAIM

THIS CERTIFIES THAT

_____

HAS THE RIGHT TO WORK SITE #_____

DATE _____

RECORDER _____

Traffic Safety

Lead Ins

- Bring a stop sign to group time and ask children to identify it. What color is it? What shape is it? What do the letters S-T-O-P spell? Where and why are stop signs posted? What other traffic signs and signals are there? Go for a walk to see what signs and signals can be spotted. Make a list for the class and add to it as more are spotted. Take pictures of them to add to the list or use the signs on pages 238–239.

- Discuss the people who have jobs helping with traffic safety. Discuss the roles of police officers, crossing guards, sheriffs, Highway Patrol officers, etc.

- Bring in a bike helmet and share it with the class. Discuss its importance. Discuss other important bike safety rules. If appropriate, offer the Bike Helmet Dot-to-Dot as an indoor extension activity (page 240).

- Bring in a variety of car seats. Try to find one for infants, one for toddlers, and one for older children. Discuss the importance of car seats and seat belts.

- Review left and right with students. Teach them the signals for left turns and right turns when driving or riding a bike. Incorporate these signs into the routine in the traffic zone outside.

- Share a driver's license with the class. If possible, enlarge it and show the different information given. Explain that driving a car (or any vehicle) is a privilege and that people have to study the laws (rules) and practice a long time before they can get a driver's license.

- Share the traffic zone and its rules with the children once it has been established outside. Explain that they will be practicing good driving skills, bike safety, and pedestrian awareness so that they can get their own (school) drivers' licenses.

- Introduce books about traffic and safety during group times.

Suggested Materials for Traffic Safety

- children's books about traffic, safety, and vehicles
- street signs (pages 238–239)
- traffic cones
- tricycles
- cars and other playground vehicles
- playground chalk, various colors
- boxes to make cars
- paint stirrers, dowels, or yardsticks
- traffic signs
- whistles for each child
- construction paper—red, yellow, blue, green
- bike helmets
- copy of the DMV driving and bike safety regulations
- posters about safety on bikes and when driving
- Traffic Zone Layout

School Zone

Traffic Safety *(cont.)*

Teacher Preparation

1. Create an outdoor traffic area using playground chalk. Draw streets with crosswalks. Create a short stretch of multi-lane highway with dashed lines dividing the lanes. Label left and right turning lanes. If tricycles and cars will be used, add a bike lane. Add signs, traffic cones, and other appropriate items.

2. Create street signs and signals. Use the signs on pages 238–239 as a guide. Enlarge and copy them onto appropriately colored paper, laminate them, and attach them to dowels, yardsticks, or paint stirrers (from a hardware store). The sticks can be placed in large buckets of wet sand or stuck down in plastic traffic cones. Hint: Introduce a few new signs each day. This will give children a chance to absorb the new information and will keep interest up.

3. Make copies of the Driver's License (page 237) and obtain pictures of each student to be added to their license once they learn their safety rules. Present students who have successfully learned traffic safety rules with certificates and official licenses.

4. Determine a maximum number of participants in the traffic zone. See what happens when the number is exceeded. Use the situation to discuss terms like *gridlock, traffic jam,* and *standstill.* Decide with students how many vehicles should be on the road at a given time for safety.

5. Set up a series of cones for children to drive or ride around to fine tune their driving skills. Model the layout after the one used by the DMV for motorcycle driving tests. (See illustration.)

6. Establish uniforms and job descriptions for the traffic safety personnel. Decide if issuing tickets will be part of the routine. If so, the tickets will have to be designed. Provide neon orange vests for the crossing guards and road workers and blue vests and hats for the police officers. Use the captain's hat on page 24 for the police officers. **Hint:** Cover the wings (insignia) before copying pattern.
   If whistles are appropriate additions to the costumes and are available for each child, label them and instruct children to keep them in their cubbies when not in use.

7. Add stories to the reading area about safety, cars and trucks, and other types of vehicles.

8. Ask a local police officer to come in and talk about bike safety, car seats, and other traffic issues important to children.

Traffic Safety *(cont.)*

Student Preparation

1. Create a sign saying, "Traffic Safety Starts Here," for the traffic zone created outside. Embellish the sign with pictures of car seats, safety signs, and bike helmets.

2. Brainstorm a list of traffic safety rules with the teacher. Include information about riding in cars and school buses, walking, and riding bikes. Create a poster listing all the "traffic safety" rules pertinent to the play yard. Post the list outside. Add to the list as the play yard is transformed into a traffic zone.

3. Make or color street signs to be used outside in the traffic zone. Draw street lines (double, single, or dashed) and color curbs to create different street patterns.

4. Study the traffic rules and practice safe riding and "driving" to get a personal driver's license. (Remember, this driver's license only means you can drive at school!)

5. Make a car using a cardboard copy paper box and the patterns on page 192–194.

Vocabulary Building

bumper-to-bumper	double	signal light
citation	grid lock	single
commuter	pedestrian	stand still
crossing guard	police officer	ticket
crosswalk	policeman	traffic jam
curved	policewoman	vehicle
dashed	rush hour	

Traffic Safety (cont.)

Literacy Development

- Create a class book of traffic safety signs. Enlarge the cards on pages 238–239, color them, and place one on each page of the book. Interview children about what each sign means and add their responses to the page. Add pictures from magazines and children's illustrations. Later, add it to the reading center.

- Talk about different words or phrases used to describe unusually slow traffic situations. Include words like *traffic jam, bumper-to-bumper, stalled, gridlock,* and *rush hour traffic.* Make a list and add to it as new phrases are heard. What words do newscasters use to describe traffic in the area?

- What does "Ped-Xing" mean? Often, people look at the sign and know what it means before actually decoding the words (Pedestrian Crossing). See what the children think. Have them sound out the letters and discuss the function of the "X" in the word. Are their other signs like this one?

- Use the driver's license as an opportunity to practice name writing and to review each child's address. As each child completes his or her driver's license, add the information regarding hair and eye color to charts.

- Play "Red Light, Green Light" with children. Add "Yellow Light" once they are comfortable playing the game. Try the game with the whole class standing in a line. Later, try the game in smaller groups with children on bikes or in cars.

- Play "Left Turn, Right Turn." To play, demonstrate how to hop, or side-step, to the left or to the right while standing. More advanced players can make a 90-degree turn to the left or the right. Make sure the children are standing at least an arm's length apart and tell them they will either be turning to the left or to the right when you call out the words. Or, you can hold up signs with L or R on them, or the words Left and Right.

Numeracy Development

- Use the charts created for eye and hair color to do math activities. Graph the numbers of each color. Determine the most and the least of each color in the class.

- Measure each child for his or her driver's license. Who is the tallest? Who is the shortest? How many children are the same height?

- Discuss and draw the different types of lines found on streets. There are double lines, single lines, and dashed lines. Try drawing street patterns and include some curvy lines. Look for pictures in magazines of different types of roads and road markings.

- Do the Bike Helmet Dot-to-Dot. Demonstrate how to make a dot-to-dot picture for a traffic cone. See if children can make their own traffic cone dot-to-dots.

- Curbs come in different colors and the colors mean different things. Start a list of curb colors and their meanings. How many can the children list? Incorporate this research into the Traffic Zone. Add curbs with 20-minute parking, no parking, etc.

- Set up different numbers of cones to maneuver through while riding bikes or driving cars. If there are 10 cones, how many turns do you make to get through them all? How many left turns and how many right turns?

- Go for a walk. Count the number of traffic signs, traffic signals, crosswalks, people wearing helmets, etc.

Traffic Safety *(cont.)*

Character Nametags

Policeman

Policewoman

Police Officer

Crossing Guard

Driver's License

Name

Address

Age	Eyes	Hair	Height

Safety Knowledge Award
Congratulations

_____

has successfully learned all the traffic safety rules.
Date:_____

Traffic Safety *(cont.)*

Traffic Sign Cards

Stop

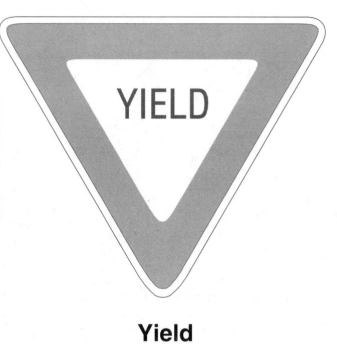

Yield

**Pedestrian
Crossing**

**Speed
Limit**

Traffic Safety *(cont.)*

Traffic Sign Cards *(cont.)*

School Zone

No Parking

Handicap Zone

Fasten Seat Belt

Traffic Safety *(cont.)*

Bike Helmet Dot-to-Dot

Begin at the star. Connect the dots from 1–10. Color in the picture.

Always wear a helmet!

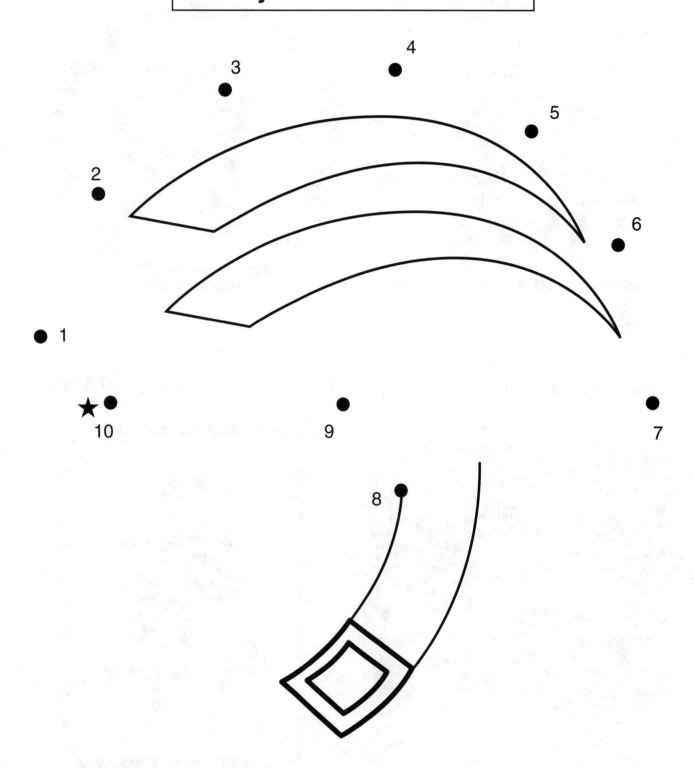

Traffic Safety *(cont.)*

Directions: Trace the dotted lines in the picture to put seatbelts on the children.

Seatbelts are Important
Always wear a seatbelt in the car!

Appendix

Numbers Cards

0	1 .
2 ••	3 •••

Appendix *(cont.)*

Numbers Cards *(cont.)*

4 ● ● ● ●	5 ● ● ● ● ●
6 ● ● ● ● ● ●	7 ● ● ● ● ● ● ●

Numbers Cards *(cont.)*

8

9

●●●●●●●●●

●●●●●●●●●●

10

●●●●●●●●●●

Open/Closed Sign

Fold the sign on the dotted lines, punch holes where indicated, and attach yarn to create a hanger. If possible, have children trace the letters of the sign.

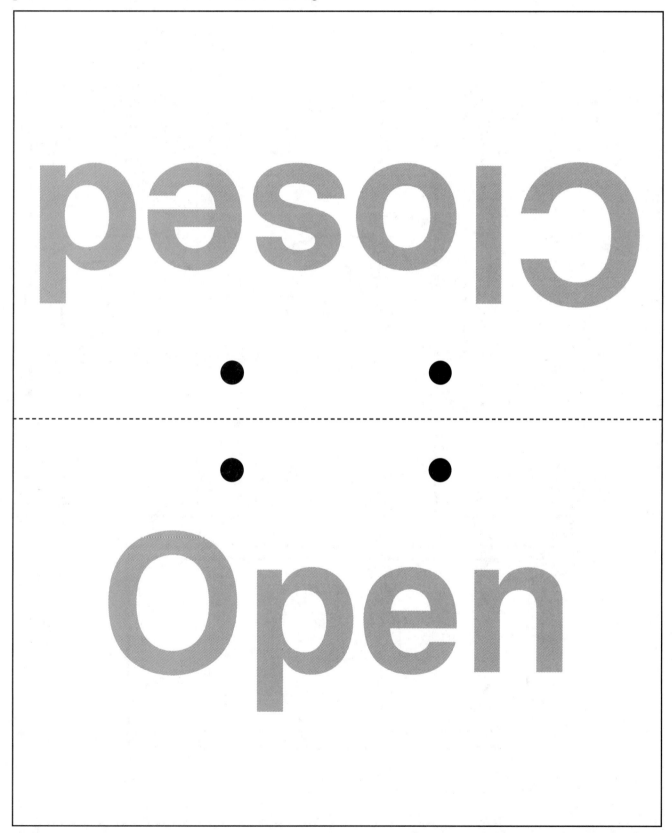

Appendix *(cont.)*

Paper Money

Copy the money onto appropriately colored paper. Adjust the size of the money to fit the center's cash register.

Appendix (cont.)

Coin Money

Copy money onto appropriately colored paper. Adjust the size of the money to fit the center's cash register.

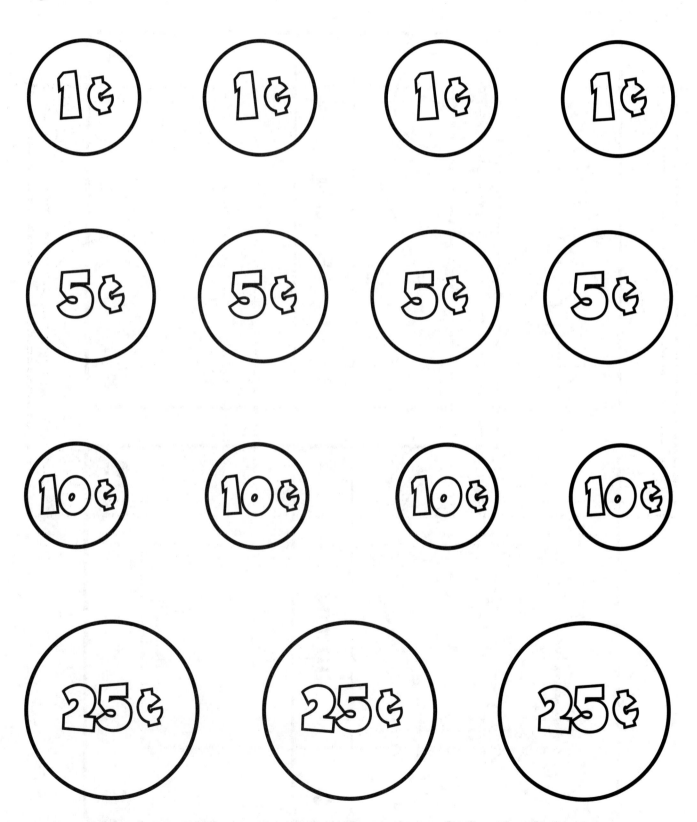

Appendix *(cont.)*

Credit Card Pattern

Copy the credit card patterns onto colored paper. Carefully fold the pattern on the dashed line and glue together using a glue stick. Have each child write his or her name on the card or draw a special picture. Laminate the cards for durability.

Appendix *(cont.)*

Checkbook Pattern

Copy the appropriate amount of checks for each checkbook. Copy the cover on a different color paper. Staple the checks together on the left side of the checkbook. Fold the cover over the checks. Help each child write his or her name on the checkbook cover.

Date

Pay to the order of _____

$

_____

Memo _____   _____

Name

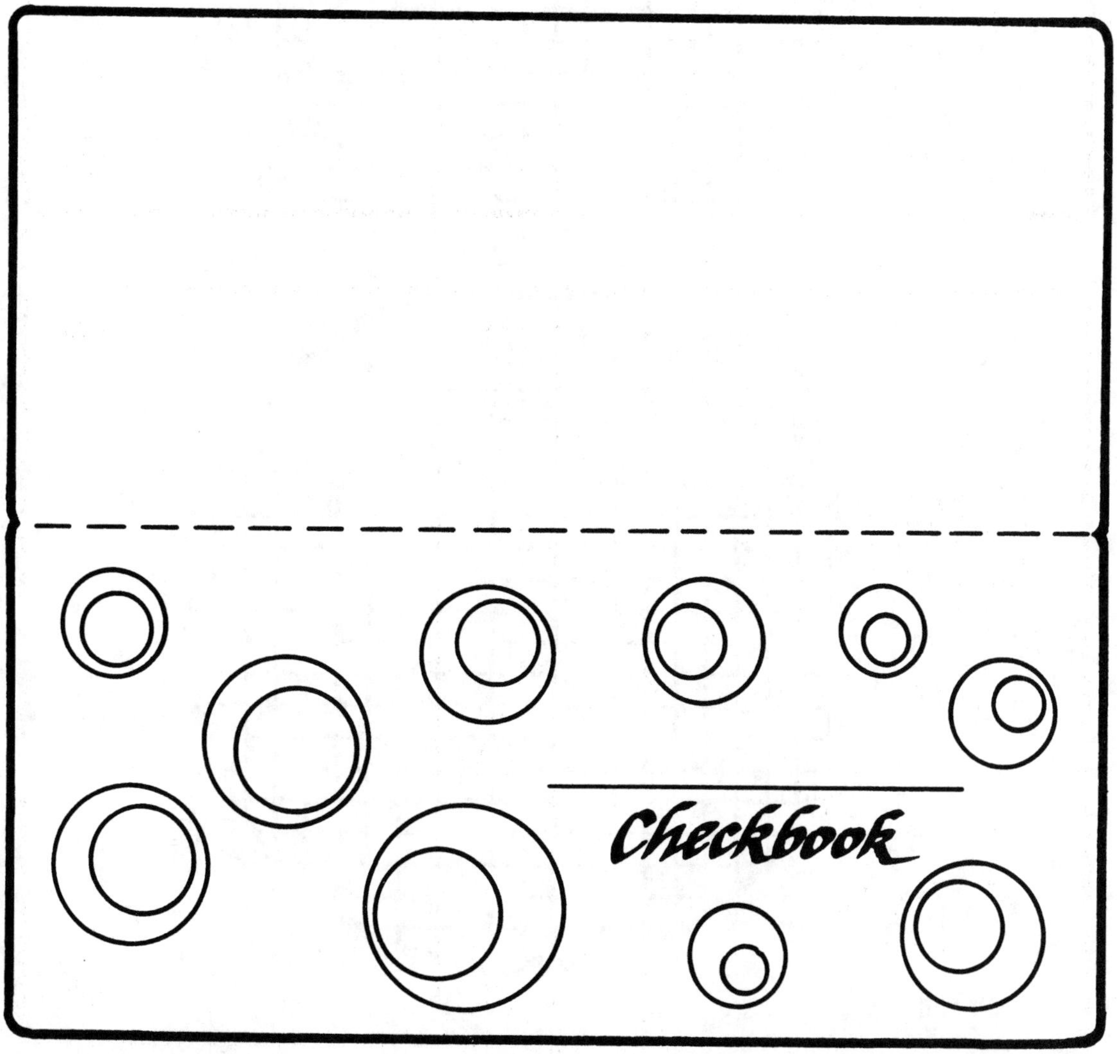

Checkbook

Appendix *(cont.)*

Microphone Pattern

Copy, cut out, and laminate the microphone pattern. Be careful not to cut the pattern on the dashed line. Fold the pattern on the dashed line. Affix the ends of the pattern to the top of a foil-covered paper towel roll.

Alternative: Attach a tennis ball or a Styrofoam ball to a toilet paper roll. Cover with aluminum foil. Add colored tape to the top and bottom for decoration.

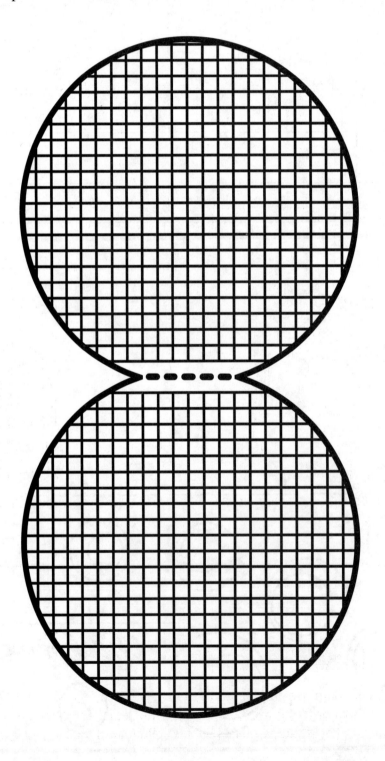

Appendix *(cont.)*

Vest Pattern

Directions: This vest idea can work for many different dramatic play centers. Use a brown or white grocery bag. The bottom sides of the bag will become the shoulders of the vest.

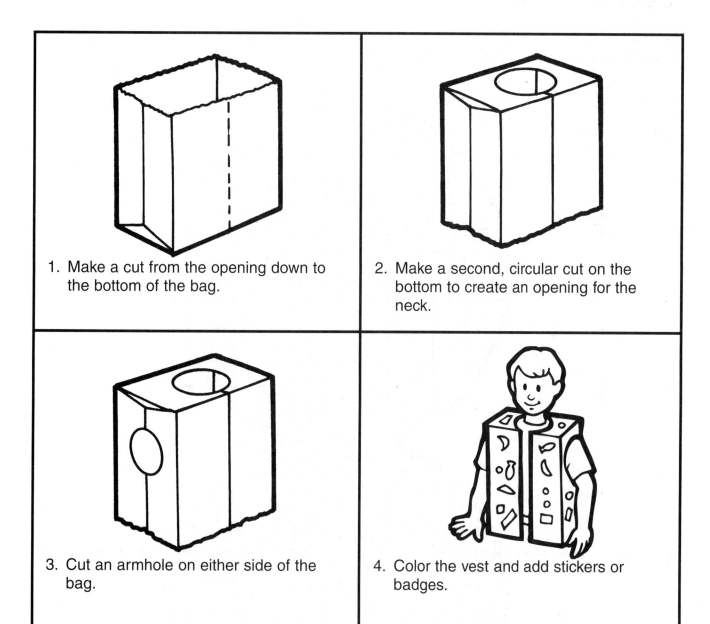

1. Make a cut from the opening down to the bottom of the bag.

2. Make a second, circular cut on the bottom to create an opening for the neck.

3. Cut an armhole on either side of the bag.

4. Color the vest and add stickers or badges.

Alternatives

- Collect old suit vests from parents or thrift shops. Dark colors work best. Decorate and label for each dramatic play center.

- Create "sandwich board" vests using felt squares. You will need two felt squares and two six-inch strips of wide ribbon or fabric for each vest. Simply attach the ribbon or fabric strips to the top of each felt square so that it can by placed over a child's head. Label as needed.

Appendix *(cont.)*

Apron Ideas

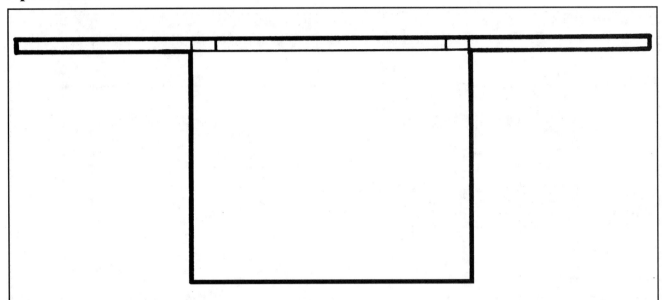

1. Create aprons using felt or vinyl fabric cut to a desired rectangular size. Attach ribbon or Velcro strips to either side of the fabric to create a simple around-the-waist apron. (See illustration.)

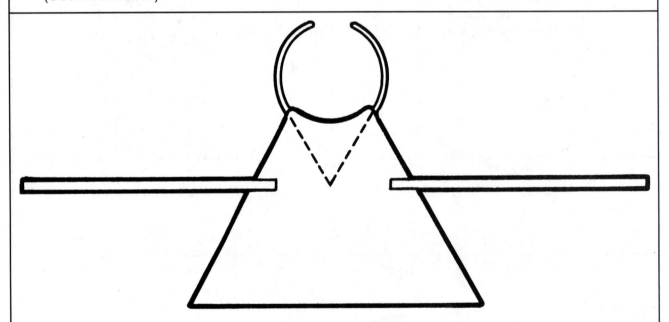

2. For a different style, cut a rectangular- or triangular-shaped piece of fabric. Attach waist ties and a neckband. To make the neckband, cut the desired length of thick yarn or twine. Tie it into a circle that will easily fit over a child's head. Lay the circle of yarn or twine on the fabric so that the top of the triangle can be folded over it. Glue or sew the fabric down, encasing the twine or yarn. (See illustration.)

Generic Labels

Room Capacity

Cash Register

Employees Only

Generic Labels *(cont.)*

Food Area

Office

 # Restroom

 # Restroom

Appendix *(cont.)*

Supplies

Work Area

Work Bench

Appendix *(cont.)*

Generic Character Nametags

Manager

 # Cashier

Customer

Owner